School Matters Foundation

www.SchoolMattersFoundation.org

CHAOS

in our schools

2nd Edition

T.L. Zempel

Federal and state mandates,
and the illogical policies that followed,
have mired everyone in nonsensical hogwash.

This is one veteran teacher's account of life in the trenches.

For my late father, William Zempel,
who taught me to do the right thing.

And for the late Dr. Molly Doll,
whose ideas continue to inspire.

Most teachers would say the best determinants
of student performance are low class size
and positive student engagement.
The latter is Edu-speak for 'no behavior problems'.

On the other hand, the education elite believe class size
and behavior are negligible in determining learning outcomes.
This is because things like class size and behavior are
simple to fix; the education elite cannot claim
expert status over them.

They've learned they can, however, convince the public
that education is far more complex than common sense
would indicate, and that the ordinary person cannot
possibly understand what the elites think they know.
Don't be fooled by their spin. The experts have
little idea how real classrooms work.

It is essential to give each student what he needs.
It is equally impossible to do that within the
current paradigm of education.

Contents

Foreword

Most of us agree that education is in trouble in our country. What we can't sort out is how to fix it. The experts have propagated numerous theories over the years, each promising to provide the last, best hope. One stand-out expert weighs in on the efficacy of these theories in the first paragraph of his op-ed that appeared in *Education Week* in 2015:

> *Let's review the educational cure-alls of past decades: back to basics, the open classroom, whole language, constructivism, and E.D. Hirsch's excruciatingly detailed accounts of what every 1st or 3rd grader should know, to name a few. It seems America's teachers and students are guinea pigs in the perennial quest for universal excellence. Sadly, though, the elusive panacea that will solve all of education's woes has remained, well, elusive.* [1]

This is from Dr. James Delisle, a noted Gifted and Talented specialist whose books appear prominently on Prufrock Press's webpages. When I read this op-ed in 2016, I thought, '*Amazing! Someone of note finally speaks the truth about teaching.*'

From a teacher's perspective, there is a disconnect between the messages routinely delivered by administration and the reality we experience in the classroom. We are continually told that if we would just latch on to 'this best practice' or 'that best practice', all our students will respond positively, and every issue in our classroom will be resolved. This fad-driven professional development creates havoc in schools and cynicism among teachers. No strategy touted by their principal is given much credence because teachers know that next year, something new will take its place.

The education elites have become fond of thrusting cutting-edge programs at us – I have manuals for many of these sitting on my shelves at home, distant memories of their tried-and-failed implementation clouding my mind. I also remember my introduction to some major requirements: **Differentiation**, **Visible Learning**, and **Common Core**, back in the school years 2012 and 2013.

In truth, teachers want to believe there is a cure-all for the malaise they see in their classrooms. But we know something the experts don't: the reality of classroom teaching.

---

[1] Dr. James Delisle, "Differentiation Doesn't Work". *Education Week*, 2015.

Where did all these education game-changers come from? Why have we been assailed over the last twenty-five years by what has become a cottage industry of re-inventing learning?

I believe we can trace it to our lawmakers.

In 1965, Congress passed the **Elementary and Secondary Education Act** (ESEA), a piece of legislation that addresses the disparities in achievement between impoverished populations and those who are not. It is where we get programs that begin with the word *Title*:

- Title I: mandated programs in low-income schools.
- Title II: funding for school libraries, textbooks, and preschool programs.
- Title III: mandates and funding for adult education.
- Title IV: $100 million over five years to fund research and training.
- Title V: grants under Public Law 874 (for Title I, to address operating costs in low-income schools).
- Title VI: definitions and limitations to the law. [2]

Every five years, this Act has supposedly been reviewed by Congress, with new legislation added periodically, such as Title IX in 1972, which prohibits sex discrimination in any program receiving federal funds. There are other extensions of the original ESEA, but for the purpose of this book, I will discuss only two of them.

In 2001, Congress worked in a bipartisan way to write a law that would become much more intrusive than any of its predecessors. Lawmakers were particularly proud of this bipartisan legislation, while educators across the country could hear alarm bells. **No Child Left Behind** (NCLB) [3] ushered in our current era of bureaucracy run amok. One of its major provisions is something called Adequate Yearly Progress, which *"allows the U.S. Department of Education to determine how every public school and school district in the country is performing academically according to results on standardized tests."* [4]

The very name *No Child Left Behind* portended positive change. Unfortunately, the law contained enough improbable-to-achieve mandates that the Dept. of Education had to establish flexibility in its implementation and waivers for its requirements. [5] The ultimate waiver came in 2009, when

---

[2] Paul, Catherine A. Elementary and Secondary Education Act of 1965.
[3] U.S. Department of Education: *No Child Left Behind*
[4] Wikipedia: *Adequate Yearly Progress*
[5] U.S. Department of Education: *ESEA Flexibility*

Congress proposed the **Every Student Succeeds Act** (ESSA), a bill that placed measuring growth in students above grade-level achievement as the arbiter of success. This is a flawed proposition on two fronts: it requires teachers to focus on activities other than teaching, and it provides false security to students and guardians regarding learning. ESSA was signed into law in 2015; while it supersedes the earlier requirements of NCLB, it does mimic many of them, such as requiring states to report on student performance and graduation rates and identify the lowest performing schools. One major departure from NCLB is that states now have the flexibility to develop their own accountability measures. [6]

In 2010, Colorado's legislature responded to ESSA by creating a law they coined **The Great Teachers and Leaders Act,** Senate Bill 10-191. From the moment it passed, districts across the state were compelled to develop teacher evaluation systems that reward compliance with mandated data collection regarding growth in student achievement.

I endured one of these evaluation schemes for five years; it seemed to have no purpose other than appeasing the legislators who drafted SB 10-191. The requirements for teachers were onerous, including the Individual Educator Goals that I describe in chapter 9. I would surmise that the way these goals were managed in my school (and likely across the district) little resembled the intent behind the protocols so carefully crafted by district officials. That's because they represented a lot of behind-the-scenes work, and when people are given onerous amounts of extra work to do – paperwork that has no bearing on any aspect of their real job – they are apt to take shortcuts.

The Great Teachers and Leaders Act was sold to the public as a **performance-based doctrine.** [7] However, half of the evaluation system required by it comes from a principal's **unaudited notes about a teacher's activities**. This is not performance; it is opinion. The rest of the evaluation is a mix of **teacher-collected data**, a **school improvement plan** drafted and graded by the principal and applied to everyone, and **aggregated test scores**, also applied to everyone. **This** is the great improvement Colorado's legislature created for its thousands of schoolchildren across the state in 2010. If you think I'm not being facetious with that statement, check Colorado's test scores for the last ten years (see page 45.)

When Congress passes massive reform legislation, especially for something like education, massive bureaucracy becomes inevitable. What we have now are well-intended but ineffective multiple layers of

---

[6] Generative AI: accessed Feb 2025.
[7] Colorado Dept. of Education: *State Model Evaluation System*. 2019. This act was introduced by our principal as *The Educator Effectiveness Act.* You can find an analysis of it at https://www.schoolmattersfoundation.org/history-behind-sb-10-191.

requirements. Federal mandates mean that states must enact their own measures, and thousands of people are hired merely to enforce compliance. Circular bureaucracy is the result.

Complex systems require complex paperwork and a whole lot of money. They also allow for the real possibility of subterfuge and even fraud among participants.

Chaos has taken over our schools:
- Illogical policies couched in pleasant language.
- Growth, whether authentic or not, considered more important than achievement.
- Administrators and teachers participating in appearance-based protocols.
- Non-teaching requirements for teachers assigned more value than actual teaching.
- Students seen more as subjects of data collection than as learners.
- School district websites filled with indoctrination and complexity.

I will address each point in this book. My own plan for improvement appears in chapter 18. If you are tempted to jump ahead, don't feel bad. Just as students are coached to look at the questions prior to reading nonfiction to get the gist of what they must know, you may benefit from seeing the endpoint I propose prior to reading the exposé that supports it.

Finally, as you prepare to delve into the darkness, consider this: our public schools are tax-supported institutions. How much do you really know about them? What can you share about the curriculum children are studying and the tests they are taking, right now? Ultimately, it is the students who are the most important part of a classroom. Ironically, that idea has been diluted in our lawmakers' attempts to improve the quality of education delivered in this country.

I share this story as a teacher who has worked in the classroom for more than thirty years. I am not an expert, just a regular person sharing the truth behind the facade. I am sure plenty of actual experts will weigh in on my claims. It is up to you to discern what to accept and what to consider with suspicion.

T.L. Zempel

CHAOS in our schools

The best way to get people, en masse, to accept
a bad situation is to sugar-coat it
with feel-good language.

This has been the case
in public education policy for decades.

Bureaucracy:

an organization that is complex with multi-layered systems and processes.[1]

---

[1] Banton, Carolyn. Bureaucracy: *Investopedia.com*. 5 Sept 2020

1 The New Normal

What does it mean to be consumed by bureaucracy?

Colorado schoolteachers have been finding out for more than a decade. Their professional lives are controlled by policies that are not only cumbersome, but deceptive as well. People outside the field do not understand the many layers behind what goes on inside our schools. Most of their information comes from political soundbites, yearly feel-good speeches, and promotions for new taxation initiatives. They have little idea how terms like *Research-Based*, *Best Practices*, and *Data-Driven* have become doublespeak. [1]

The paradigm of education in Colorado has shifted since 2012. Because of Senate Bill 10-191, enacted into law in 2011, documentation and data collection have eclipsed instruction as the primary focus in a teacher's career. Of course, this is not what the legislature intended, by any means. It is what happens, however, when people try to fix something by attacking its periphery rather than its roots. Here is an introduction to that mandate, as described on the Colorado Department of Education's (CDE's) website:

> Senate Bill 10-191 changes the way all educators (principals/assistant principals, teachers, and special service providers) will be evaluated in Colorado, with the ultimate goal of continuously supporting educators' professional growth and, in turn, accelerating student results.
>
> The new evaluation requirements include opportunities for reflection, review, professional development, and growth. SB 10-191 requirements include:
> - Annual evaluation for all principals/assistant principals, teachers and special service providers.

---

[1] Doublespeak: deliberately euphemistic, ambiguous, or obscure language. The term is a hybrid of two terms made up by George Orwell for his book *1984:* "doublethink" and "newspeak".

- Evaluation based on statewide Quality Standards defining what it means to be an effective teacher, principal/assistant principal, or special service provider; the professional practice Quality Standards account for half of an educator's annual evaluation
- Non-probationary status is earned after three consecutive years of demonstrating effectiveness
- Non-probationary status is lost after two consecutive years of less than effective ratings. [2]

At first glance, the above bullet points might sound reasonable. Evaluating teachers on their performance using standards everyone can agree on seems like a good idea, because what teachers do is crucial to the development of future generations of citizens. We all know that. Most of us also suspect there are some teachers who are just skating by.

The solution to that is not in creating a massive bureaucracy to force quality in education. The fallout from attempting this has included unintended consequences, the worst of which is that the evaluation systems created to comply with SB 10-191 are laden with requirements that remove teaching as the primary focus of teachers.

The new reality we are faced with, as teachers, is that it
is more important to talk strategically about teaching
and to report on our efforts than to teach.

Teachers are rewarded, monumentally, for completing two activities: *collecting data* and *documenting instruction*. In fact, the more a teacher documents her classroom activities, the more likely it is that a principal will give her that favorable review, regardless of what he has witnessed himself.

In the spring of 2017, I took my assistant principal up on his invitation to provide documented evidence that would refute any rating on his final evaluation. (He provided this opportunity to all his teachers.) Looking back through my digital notes, I found the evidence I needed, and he did change his marks from effective to highly effective on three indicators of performance. He had no idea, however, *when* I had completed that documentation or *if* it represented anything that had really happened. For all he knew, I could have looked at his preliminary findings, determined what might change his mind, and added notes to my year-long handwritten plan book, a document that is

---

[2] SB 10-191: Senate Bill 10-191. https://www.cde.state.co.us/educatoreffectiveness/sb-policy, Updated 2018

considered to have legal merit. This is a big deal. Think about the ramifications of placing such stock in documented 'evidence'.

There is no nice way to say it: our schools have become havens for subterfuge, and our teachers have, for years, been saddled with pointless and redundant requirements in their jobs.

How did we get here? It has been an amazingly short journey, traveled in purposeful stages over only a few years. Once the directive was issued via legislation, school districts jumped into overdrive and the changes began their rollout in the fall of 2012.

Our current path began with the idea of growth. As teachers, we all agree that growth is essential. If we're not growing, we're stagnating. The focus on studying growth as a strategy to meet student need did not ring alarm bells for many of us at first. We had been casually studying this information annually since first administering CSAP in 2001.[3] We used what we learned to adjust our teaching strategies, informally, because that's what teachers do.

In 2012, analyzing growth in standardized test scores became tracking growth in our own classrooms.

We were informed that the growth demonstrated by our students is so important it eclipses their grade-level achievement. Any analysis of test results should focus on the growth from one year to the next rather than the raw score itself. The new teacher evaluation system would rely, in part, on this rationale. However, because it is not possible to include standardized test scores as part of a *formal* evaluation, a system that *could* be doable by every teacher had to be developed.[4]

In came a plan requiring all teachers to create learning goals for our students, goals that we could then track for growth across a school year. In effect we were creating *our own* testing vehicle, vetted by no one but our principal or her designee. At the end of the school year, the growth we reported would influence our evaluation by 15% (in the early years) and give some teachers a bonus for exceptional performance. It became clear early on that our data *wouldn't* need to be verified by anyone other than ourselves.[5]

[3] Colorado Student Assessment Program (CSAP): Colorado's State standardized test from 1997-2011; completed in March each year.
[4] Not all students took CSAP; only those in grades 3 – 7 and 10 did. Additionally, the unions had resisted rating teaching according to test results for decades.
[5] See chapter 7, page 67, for how data collection was first presented to us.

In early 2014, I began to wonder how far up the ladder this practice of rewarding growth went. So I looked at the CDE's website to find the full wording of the new law. I discovered that SB 10-191 was not only a performance mandate for **teachers** but for **principals** as well. All of us were evaluated annually by *someone*. We all had to document and collect data to prove our worth.

Were principals creating and tracking growth goals for their teachers like those we made for our students? Were my colleagues and I the unwitting participants in another person's *own* growth data?

Our principal had shared the new evaluation rubric with us; we knew that part of our evaluation pie was labeled *School Improvement Plan*. How was that measured? I wondered what *her* evaluation rubric looked like. I knew a teacher's data could be suspect; it was not difficult to imagine a similar scenario for our administrators.

Where were the checks and balances? What about the children we were charged with teaching? Did anyone care that they no longer appeared to matter? The policies foisted on us in 2012 became the new normal in our careers. Teachers were consumed with the protocols to receive a favorable evaluation to the extent that our students moved to the periphery of our efforts. This became the elephant in the room that no one addressed, ever.

I was inspired to write my first book, *Finishing School*, as a way to deal with the absurdities of this new world. I labeled it fiction, but it was an account of many actual events in my school between 2012 and 2014. Read on for the story behind the story.

How We Got Here

Experiences make the man, a wise man once said. It's hard to divorce one from the other, and probably not advisable.

In my first interview for a teaching job in 1987, I remember answering a stock question about my motivation like this: *"I want to help children reach their potential, and I have a feeling there are a lot of disenfranchised kids out there. I wish to bridge the gap between those who know they can and those who think they can't."*

I wonder how many elites in education today remember answering a question like that similarly? It appears that the grab for power and accolades has eclipsed many a pristine motivation. One principal told me proudly that he had spent only three years in a classroom before becoming a principal, which he had been doing ever since, around 30 years. He also felt no compassion for his teachers: He said it was utter nonsense that current teachers cannot manage to do what he did, with great success and 45 students, in 1979. If teachers can't hack it, they shouldn't be in the profession.

Those are the kind of statements used to keep teachers in line. Gaslight them; make them feel incompetent because they find it challenging to manage children who were raised by smart devices and a babysitter called YouTube. Point out that the Best Practices praised by John Hattie and company work marvelously in videos, so why are teachers having trouble? Insist that the only thing standing between a teacher and her students' success is her own laziness and/or incompetence.

If these assertions possessed validity, our education story would probably be different. But our story is not different. Almost no one is happy with the path public education is on. Politicians and district officials think they can improve outcomes by requiring more non-teaching activities from teachers. The experts think *they* can improve instruction by proposing strategies and programs while ignoring the realistic implementation of them.

What the people in power don't want to understand is that programs, strategies, and teacher evaluation schemes will not fix the education problem in this country. Strategies require personnel to administer them, and the way that personnel has been deployed does not work. Throwing more requirements at teachers won't make it work.

Have you ever thought about what it takes to be a teacher? You have a job that puts you on stage for 7 hours a day. (If you don't like your audience, it's even harder.) The best part about teaching is working with the children. Ironically, it can also be the worst.

Teachers also deal with the public perception that they have an easy job. Even when public figures applaud us with condescending statements like, "We owe our teachers a debt of gratitude...", many in their audience are thinking, 'Yeah, but they get to leave at 3:00 and they have summers off.'

It's hard to combat that kind of thinking when it's true.

We do have enviable 'office' hours. We do have school vacations that other workers in America don't get. We wish everyone wasn't jealous of us, but we don't dwell on it.

There is, of course, more to it than that. Being a supervisor to people who need a great deal of supervision is wearing on a person. And the fatigue is cumulative. The biggest shock to new teachers is usually how tired they are, all the time.

Your first three years as a teacher feel impossible; you wonder what made you think you could do this job. Especially when your college education did not wholly prepare you for it. You don't want to quit, however. This was your dream. You had such excellent teachers in elementary school that you wanted to be one yourself. And gradually, you find your groove. You amass materials and experience that is priceless. You begin to enjoy the new challenges that come along.

Then the change begins. It happens in stages, with a summer break to disguise the reality. At first, the changes are not intrusive. You spend a half-day at the beginning of a school year examining and discussing how students did the previous year on CSAP. As a grade-level team, you decide what instruction in reading and writing your incoming sixth graders are going to need most. You make notes in your plan book, and everyone generally agrees that descriptive writing or being able to make inferences could use some emphasis in your instruction.

After this, you go back to your classroom and pull out the resources you've accumulated to see what might work. You also research on the internet, and when you find something that looks useful, you email a link to your colleagues. It's all an enjoyable process, and you congratulate yourself on your career choice that has given you so much to like about the job you do every day.

Then, you realize the changes *have* become intrusive. You wonder why everyone seems so stressed all the time, and why questions such as *"Why are we doing this? Who will be looking at it? Does anyone really think this will help children?"* are dodged by your principal and her staff.

You don't worry too much. You've seen other fads come and go. This one likely will, too. The next year, though, the changes have been woven into your formal evaluation. While you are nervous about that, the concept is presented in such a *'This will help your practice'* way, that you resolve to deal with it. You begin to function daily in a survival mentality. You wonder if the principal and those above her realize the significance of what they are saying. At faculty meetings, you voice your concerns to your colleagues, quietly of course, to gauge if anyone else sees the potential for fraud. You take notes in those meetings and do your best to get on board with the new routines. You try to understand why absolute uniformity is necessary, and how it can possibly mesh with differentiation. And you wonder, briefly, what it would take to change career paths. But then you realize you are unfit for any other career.

You also realize that even though teaching has become nonsensical, it is your comfort zone, and you still love it. You cannot contemplate doing anything else.

Why the Backlash Against Teachers?

Teaching is a very independent profession. Once you close that door, you're the master of your domain. For the most part, elementary teachers have been able to run their classrooms exactly as they wish, with little interference from their principal. But what did that look like? For some teachers, it was a mix of activities: direct instruction, independent work, small group tutoring, and lots of enrichment. For others, however, it was all direct instruction with a lot of silent seatwork, and almost nothing enriching. Every school has some of these teachers, and every parent does their best to keep their child from ending up in that classroom.

Principals who wanted to sway the balance of teaching strategies in their schools toward research-based models would do their best to preach, but their sermons often fell on deaf ears. Teachers of the old guard would sit through their required professional development, participating minimally, and then return to their classrooms and continue with business as usual. There was nothing the principal could do. The evaluation of teachers was mostly ornamental.

When I was hired by my Colorado district in 1998, I attended new teacher orientations weekly that first year. At the start, the HR lady in charge told us that all we had to do was get through our first three years and one day without a blemish, and we were set for life. We had reached non-probationary status, effectively, tenure.

Try to imagine being a teacher who went into teaching for love of children and learning. This news filled you with relief. You knew that teaching was going to be a hard job, but you had weighed the pros and cons and still felt you had made the right choice. At least now you wouldn't have to deal with unnecessary headaches in trying to keep the job you were so committed to.

Now imagine you are a teacher who *didn't* have high ideals in mind. Uppermost for you is that it is an easy job, with summers off. You can do anything in your room with impunity once you pass that probationary stage. You see your job as assigning work to students and keeping their parents off your back. Your students sit quietly and do that work. You go home happy every day, congratulating yourself on the excellent career choice you made. Of course, you must put on the occasional dog-and-pony show for your principal when he visits once in a blue moon. But that's okay. You've put in the work to curry favor with him; you say the right things at the right time and make it look as if you are "strict" because that's good for kids. They need structure.

Occasionally, you run across a principal who doesn't buy into your hogwash, but that doesn't really matter. You haven't committed a felony. There's nothing he can do. If you continue to say you are 'working on his suggestions', you will skate by. If your principal *really* doesn't like you, he will play hardball: transfer you to another school.

This doesn't eliminate the problem, of course. It becomes someone else's. Whenever a new teacher was transferred to our school, the first thing I asked the secretary, under the table, was, "Voluntary or involuntary transfer?" And I wondered what negotiations went on behind the scenes in these trade-offs.

I worked with one of these horrible teachers for ten years. I even sat on her interview committee. She said all the right things, and I felt pretty good about having her join our team. Once she got the job, however, she behaved very differently from how she had presented herself. (This is why I have zero confidence in teacher interviews.)

When the principal was around, she did and said everything right for three years. Almost from the start, however, I could see issues looming in how she talked about children: *"These kids think everything is about them. And their parents are even worse."* She also groused about the workload, and I wondered, *'What workload? You assign worksheets to kids all day and sit at your desk to grade them as they come in.'* As far as I could tell, she delivered very few lessons. (Believe me, kids talk.)

For ten years, everyone endured her presence, and when she retired (after 'buying up' all the retirement years she could because this stacks your pension) I wanted to sing "Ding-dong, the witch is dead" at her retirement party.[6]

Those in the upper echelons of education have always known teachers like this could fly under the radar. Other teachers were aware, as well. Even the public knew it through experience or hearsay.

It was stupidly easy to be a bad teacher.

---

[6] She was a second-career teacher, so retiring after ten to fifteen years was typical. She then collected two pensions.

And it was also bound to happen that the politicians would get involved... again. In 2010, the Colorado's General Assembly wrote a senate bill our principal called *The Educator Effectiveness Act*. (I have since also heard it called *The Great Teachers and Leaders Act*.) This law made it necessary for teachers to prove their worth annually, through "performance-based" protocols. In effect, tenure was to be eliminated, and pay-for-performance installed. The hope, I am sure, is that it would encourage early retirements and weed out those who found teaching an easy way to get a paycheck and, eventually, a pension. [7]

This law infiltrated our college prep programs as well. One of my young teacher friends showed me the notebook she had compiled for her own teacher prep (circa 2015) in Colorado, and I was astounded at the amount of work it represented. She had case studies, a dossier of professional techniques she had researched and practiced, and lesson plans for every nuance of differentiation one could possibly imagine. It was nothing like my easy teacher prep in the early 80's. In addition, she had to pass the PRAXIS battery of tests. [8]

What I knew about PRAXIS is that it was supposed to be very hard. I had never taken it, having been grandfathered in to Colorado teaching licensure.

Given what my friend told me about this test and her self-made teaching bible, I felt certain it was the intention of the Colorado legislature to weed out poor teaching candidates at the college level.

In November 2011, SB 10-191 passed. Early retirements did, indeed, begin their bloom. The witch retired the following spring.

---

[7] The Colorado legislature was also responding to mandates issued via *No Child Left Behind* (2001) and the *Every Student Succeeds Act* (2009).
[8] Praxis Tests: https://www.ets.org/praxis

Our rapidly moving, information-based society badly needs people who know how to find facts rather than memorize them, and who know how to cope with change in creative ways.

You don't learn those things in school.[9]

– Wendy Priesnitz

[9] Pearce,. *101 Quotes About Unschooling, Education, and Lifelong Learning.* 12 Mar 2020 in Kyle *DIY Genius*

2 Differentiation

Since the 1990's, at least, experts have been touting strategies like exploration, discussion, collaboration, differentiation, and metacognition as the way to achieve success with students.

To be sure, most teachers understand that these strategies, combined with *some* parts of direct instruction, are the most effective way to educate our young. It is not the purpose of this book to convince you otherwise. Instead, my hope is that the full picture of what teachers are up against will help you understand why strategies alone won't make the needed change for our students.

The years 2012-14 were pivotal at my school, where I taught for 20 years. In those two school years, the following requirements were foisted on us: Differentiation, Visible Learning, The Common Core, Collaboration, Documentation, Goal Setting and Growth Tracking. The mantra became *'adjust and adapt'*.

In May 2012, the teachers in my school were given a book and directed to read it over the summer, in preparation for modifying our classroom instruction the following year.

If you are a teacher, you are likely familiar with this book or another in its series, for it is *the* model for differentiation in teaching. The book we were given is called *Fulfilling the Promise of the Differentiated Classroom*, by Carol Ann Tomlinson.

For reference, Dr. Tomlinson has made a name for herself in education research since the 1980's. Her studies appear in numerous textbooks and are touted as the standard against which all programs claiming to differentiate education should be judged. Dr. Tomlinson is a featured author and member of ASCD, an organization that, according to its website, *"empowers educators to achieve excellence in learning, teaching, and leading so that every child is healthy, safe, engaged, supported, and challenged."* [1]

Wikipedia provides this background on ASCD:

[It] has more than 125,000 members from more than 128 countries, including superintendents, principals, teachers, professors of education, and other educators.

...In March 2007, ASCD launched its Whole Child Initiative to ensure all children are healthy, safe, engaged in learning, supported by caring adults, and academically challenged. [2]

This initiative influenced the trajectory of education because it spoke volumes to the power structure across the country. Dr. Tomlinson's ideas were given new credence: school districts began taking a fresh look at differentiation as a best practice.

A glimpse at the *Table of Contents* offers a snapshot of Dr. Tomlinson's philosophy:

1. What's Behind the Idea of Differentiated Classrooms?
2. Student Needs as the Impetus for Differentiation
3. Teacher Response to Student Needs: A Starting Point for Differentiation
4. Teacher Response to Student Needs: Rationale to Practice
5. Curriculum and Instruction as the Vehicle for Responding to Student Needs
6. Curriculum and Instruction as the Vehicle for Responding to Student Needs: Rationale to Practice
7. The Simple, Hard Truth About Teaching [3]

Her approach places student need in the forefront of teacher consideration. Tomlinson uses the words **Focused, Engaging, Demanding, and Scaffolded** to help teachers understand their responsibility. Additionally, she discusses creating a productive classroom environment: how communication happens, what fosters positive experiences, how decisions are made, and what the routines should be. [4]

---

[1] ASCD: Association for Supervision and Curriculum Development; https://www.ascd.org/
[2] Wikipedia: *Association for Supervision and Curriculum Development*
[3] Tomlinson, Carol Ann. *Fulfilling the Promise of the Differentiated Classroom: Strategies and Tools for Responsive Teaching*, 2003.
[4] *Fulfilling the Promise*, pp. 37-46.

Children are not just students under our charge. They are learners whose readiness for tackling the next concept must be *individually* determined. Readiness is the hallmark of differentiation, according to Tomlinson. Trying to teach children something they are not ready for is bound to be largely unsuccessful. How do teachers determine that readiness? They continually observe their students, looking for clues to well-being and cognitive development.

With differentiation, teachers must figure out what engages each student and teach to that engagement. They must bring to the table multiple ways of motivating each student. Think about the planning involved in that. Nothing is tackled without serious analysis.

Tomlinson herself has worked with students in research settings for decades, amassing data that supports her theories. Through that research, she has come to accept the following:

- What we study is essential to the structure of the discipline.
- What we study provides a roadmap toward expertise in a discipline.
- What we study is essential to building student understanding.
- What we study balances knowledge, understanding, and skill. [5]

Any instruction delivered to children must convince them that we wholly support these ideas, as well.

Her big thing, though, is to get teachers to think differently about *how* children learn. If we want the learning to stick, it must be memorable to them. It must become something they can access easily in their memory stores. Our principal put it to us this way: will students remember it for 40 *minutes*? For 40 *days*? Or, for 40 *years*. We need to aim for the *years*. Take reading instruction, for example. Teachers understand that students need to be guided to learn how to become good readers and have traditionally worked with small groups of children at their reading tables, teaching concepts that promote vocabulary development and comprehension.

Tomlinson says that is not enough. We haven't made the skills meaningful to children. They are not memorable yet. The child will not be able to access the learning in a different context.

To counteract this, Dr. Tomlinson promotes something called *metacognition*, which means 'thinking about thinking'. Teachers must teach students to understand *why* they think *what* they think. Tomlinson suggests

---

[5] *Fulfilling the Promise*, p. 60.

techniques to get this to happen, such as training kids to self-monitor their learning, track their own progress, and write reflections on what the learning really means. The theory is that when students reflect, they are more likely to learn deeply, in a way that will stick, because they understand not only the material itself, but also what they think about that material and why it is important.

How do you implement metacognition effectively? It requires trust and cooperation from the students, for one thing. It also requires a lot of time spent with each child.

Many of us sat in our meetings wondering how we could carry this off. We *wanted* to establish ties with our students based on their individual dreams and needs. We *wanted* to embrace Dr. Tomlinson's philosophies and practices.

I could see issues looming with feasibility, however.

Dr. Tomlinson could, as well:

> Teaching asks us to do the impossible. It asks us to establish ties with each child, not to establish ties with all the children as if they were one student. They are not...
>
> ...The truth is, we will never really do all each child needs us to do. A simultaneous truth is that the first truth is no reason to stop trying. [6]

Fulfilling the Promise is a book of ideas and ideals, and lots of encouragement. One might even call it inspirational. It was obvious Dr. Tomlinson cares deeply about children, and that speaks to the core of us:

> Differentiated instruction is responsive instruction. It occurs as teachers become increasingly proficient in understanding their students as individuals. [7]

The feasibility of creating individual learning platforms for every student, however, has not been seriously addressed by anyone of note.

While assuring us that her ideas are sound and have proven research behind them, Dr. Tomlinson acknowledges that she has conducted that research in controlled settings: either one-on-one or with very small groups.

That's not how real teaching works.

The fall-out from trying to teach to each child's differences is that we experience limited results and often, failure, because there are so many students, and they are all so .... different. Best practices in education may

---

[6] *Fulfilling the Promise*, p. 22
[7] *Fulfilling the Promise*, p.3

have changed for the better over the years, but how we put kids together in classrooms has not.

This sentiment is not well-received by administration. If one is caring enough, organized enough, strict enough, and competent enough, all students will respond positively to *any* strategy. End of story.

This lecture is delivered by someone who has not worked in a classroom in years, perhaps decades even. The last time this person taught, differentiation was a mostly ignored fad.

When teachers contemplate working with children, we tend to focus on the rose-colored version. Every teacher imagines her entire class so enthralled with learning that nothing ever goes awry. It's a heady feeling, imagining teaching like this in a room full of eager students.

The reality is often far different. If you are lucky, a third of your students are eager. Others harbor a hate for school because it takes effort, or it takes away from their free time, or they don't see the value in learning something they will never use in life, or they are in a perpetual power struggle with the world.

Still others have trouble retaining concepts, so they give up and often become behavior issues. And then there are those who suffer from neglect at home, so they arrive at school ill-prepared for anything but daily survival. In differentiation, teachers must accept this and adapt everything in the classroom for every possible nuance that students bring to the table. It's not doable, but you begin to doubt every skill you ever had because your principal keeps insisting that it *is* doable, bringing district experts in every now and then to punctuate her case.

This is gaslighting 101 because anyone who has worked in a classroom, especially recently, knows that effective differentiation faces two significant roadblocks:

range of abilities and class size.

The experts don't want anyone to dwell on class size because it defeats their purpose of convincing us that *methods and curriculum* alone are the foolproof way to get students to achieve. School officials jump onto this philosophy because it works better for their budget.

Around 2001, I was discussing the idea of class size with one of my brothers and mentioned that I was teaching 32 sixth graders that year. My brother, not an educator, was stunned and said, "How do you make sure everyone is learning?" I had smiled and shrugged, not wanting to admit that I couldn't.

The other aspect, the idea that *range of abilities* in a group of learners could have a significant effect on their education, has been consistently disparaged by nearly every expert and school official since the dawn of time. One significant detractor of this premise is Dr. James Delisle, a prominent GT educator and author, who wrote an op-ed about it in 2015:

> The biggest reason differentiation doesn't work, and never will, is the way students are deployed in most of our nation's classrooms. Toss together several students who struggle to learn, along with a smattering of gifted kids, while adding a few English-language learners and a bunch of academically average students and expect a single teacher to differentiate for all of them.
>
> That is a recipe for academic disaster if ever I saw one. Such an admixture of students with varying abilities in one classroom causes even the most experienced and conscientious teachers to flinch, as they know the task of reaching each child is an impossible one.... Differentiation in practice is harder to implement in a heterogeneous classroom than it is to juggle with one arm tied behind your back.[8]
>
> -   *Dr. James Delisle*

A heterogeneous classroom mixes kids together, regardless of ability, special need, behavior, or motivation. The theory is that kids will help each other, learn from each other, and grow to the best of their ability. In practice, that is not what usually happens.

The advanced students are designated as tutors for other students. (Most of the time, they reject this role, especially after trying it and realizing it's very hard.) The best-behaving students become buffers for the worst behaving. Struggling learners get the bulk of the teacher's attention because she knows it is in her best interests. Those who are already proficient can be ignored because they will do just fine on the state test.

Each of these children needs a program that challenges him *specifically*. The likelihood of that happening in a classroom of 30 to 1 is low. In this classroom, a teacher implements differentiation in a type-casting way: how likely is it to be successful, based on kid motivation, parent influence, cognitive development, and behavior? This, of course, is not the premise of differentiation. One does not choose a smaller group within one's classroom to apply it to. But teachers figure out a compromise so they can apply these

---

[8] Delisle, James. "Differentiation Doesn't Work". *Education Week*. 2015.
GT: Gifted and Talented education.

ideals to those most likely to benefit. They don't see differentiation as all or nothing.

Dr. Tomlinson's concepts would be more likely to occur if the levels of aptitude in any classroom were more closely matched. In a sixth-grade class packed with ELL and IEP students, average learners, and gifted thinkers, the cognitive levels present could range from first to eighth grade. No teacher can be an expert in meeting that wide range of needs. [9]

The opposite of a heterogeneous classroom is a homogeneous classroom, one that combines learners of like abilities. Dr. Delisle advocates this for GT. My own specialty is also gifted learners, and I know they do need a different approach. Their brains are wired at a much earlier age than the average learner to think divergently. They can often self-teach just from looking at the topic you have posted on the board. The inbred curiosity they experience about the world around them inspires them to research on their own. They also have social and emotional needs that differ from average learners. Try to imagine being able to understand the scientific ramifications of the plastic 'island' floating in the Pacific Ocean prior to being able to deal with that knowledge emotionally. [10]

It stymies me that in pushing differentiation in our schools, it never includes the gifted learners. What they need is a space of their own, unhampered by people who need babysitting. That is not what they get.

Gifted learners often experience boredom in regular classes because there is not enough stimulation in the realm of critical and divergent thinking. They are often labeled troublemakers because of their tendency to cut to the chase. My character Nick in *Finishing School* is one of these kids. Of course, because they are children, they don't realize why they feel so out of place. The Bill Gates, Steve Jobses, and Elon Musks of the world often languish in regular classrooms because their teachers neglect their need to explore, research, and study in an open-ended way.

These children also almost never get to discuss concepts with learners of a similar intellect, or probe without feeling like they must drag people behind them.

Unless a school is designated as a Gifted and Talented hub (as in my former district), administrators sprinkle these children among every

---

[9] ELL: English Language Learners; IEP: Individualized Education Program (special education)
[10] Look up pictures of the Great Pacific Garbage Patch; it is three times the size of France.

classroom in a grade level. Teachers are admonished to find ways to enrich the regular material for the advanced learners, or to create independent learning tracks just for them.

Why? Why isn't it the norm in every school to place these similarly advanced students in an environment *with someone who specializes* in working with them? If we do not effectively cultivate the intellect of the most gifted among us, how will we meet the challenges of an increasingly complex world?

But most schools don't put these children together, and we owe a lot of that mindset to the teachers' unions. For decades, they have resisted the idea of assigning students (*and* teachers) to classrooms that match their intellect and ability, interpreting egalitarianism in ways that work against learning. [11]

Even worse, many teachers put these dispersed gifted learners in charge of other learning groups in their classrooms, expecting that their expertise will help everyone else catch up.

Advanced thinkers need to be with other advanced thinkers; they challenge each other. They can express a concept in a few words and wait for the others to get that 'ah ha!' expression on their faces. This doesn't usually happen in mixed ability groups. Everyone moves at the pace of the slowest member. The learners who are not advanced must have an exceptional sense of self-worth and motivation to successfully co-learn with those who are way beyond them intellectually.

Even without the input from the unions, homogeneous grouping of advanced learners has mostly been eschewed by experts for decades now, because the education elite have research to prove that all children excel when they are put together in mixed-ability groups.

I have research from my own classroom that proves advanced thinkers who are put with people they like in mixed-ability groups dumb themselves down. A classroom *is* a "group". Just being in the same room with his best friend, a below-average achiever, caused one of my most advanced students to consistently pretend he did not understand the math concepts I was teaching.

It was maddening to me, because I could tell what he was doing. During lessons, he would look at his friend, trying to match his demeanor. He never wanted to work with anyone else, even though I tried separating them during independent practice. So, I gave up and just allowed them to be work

---

[11] Egalitarianism: the doctrine that people are equal and deserve equal rights and opportunities. *Oxford Languages.* https://languages.oup.com/google-dictionary-en/

partners; at least no one else's learning was affected by their shenanigans. My advanced thinker did not help his friend; he lagged *with* his friend. If these boys had been placed in classrooms that met their needs, they each could have grown measurably. Instead, they were enabled to focus only on their social bond, to the exclusion of their education.

The only arena where homogeneous grouping is still acceptable is in special education classrooms (also called Resource Rooms), and even those are mostly pull-out programs. The special ed students are still part of a heterogeneous classroom, but for parts of their day (for reading and math instruction, for instance) they report to the special ed teacher for direct, focused instruction that specifically addresses their IEP. [12] Over the last decade, however, teachers have been encouraged to bring the special ed teacher into *their* room, so that the special ed students don't feel the stigma of being pulled out.

Once again, in theory this sounds like a good idea. In practice, it is not. If they are to learn, students must remain focused on instruction. Students with cognitive disabilities typically have a tough time with focus even in quiet environments. Now they are sitting with their teacher in a fishbowl? It would make more sense for these kids to get their instruction in the quiet classroom that has been given to the SpEd teacher for just this purpose. But the experts think they know better.

I walked into a colleague's room one time when the SpEd teacher was also in there giving instruction at her little table, and the pandemonium of activity was not conducive to focus, let alone skill acquisition.

There is no useful reason homogeneous grouping should be so frowned upon. We're talking about *learning*...not attending a sporting event. Children's needs cannot be met if they cannot be adequately addressed. In that classroom I described earlier, the one that contains 30 children of multiple abilities and disabilities, differentiation is not happening across the board.

Oh, sure...teachers are creating *documentation* to show that it is, almost constantly. They must if they are to receive their favorable rating. Principals rely on teachers for this documentation so they can fill out their *own* paperwork, which includes rating each teacher on a long list of performance indicators. [13]

---

[12] Wikipedia: The Individualized Education Program (IEP) is a legal document under United States law; it is developed for each child in the U.S. who has tested into special services.
[13] That list can be found on page 122 or in Appendix A on page 216.

The savvy teacher soon learns that whatever the principal writes on her final evaluation will be changed if she supplies evidence that it must. If she's *really* seasoned, she spends her time writing documentation to *specifically address* that list of performance indicators. Principals understand the power of the unions; they know that refuting a teacher's documentation opens a can of worms they would rather remain closed. My own evaluator, even while not liking me, had taken my documentation seriously enough in 2017 to change his ratings on three performance indicators.

Differentiation in mixed ability and mainstreamed classrooms is a façade. It doesn't happen as teachers make it appear that it does. Doublespeak had been the norm for decades when officials discussed *special education's* effectiveness (and most teachers quietly acknowledge this), but now subterfuge regarding *all* teaching has entered the arena. At this moment, we are all culpable: teachers, administrators, and district and state officials.

Dr. Tomlinson's ideas are what we want for our kids, there is no doubt about that. Her words should be the grounding force in effective instruction:

> Teachers must take into account *who* they are teaching as well as *what* they are teaching. The goal of a differentiated classroom is to plan actively and consistently to help each learner move as far and as fast as possible along a learning continuum.

Toward that end, *we* must provide the following for each of our learners:

- ✓ purpose;
- ✓ opportunity;
- ✓ challenge;

    and

- ✓ curriculum that is important.[14]

These are the traits of education we want all our students to appreciate and accept, and it is incumbent upon us to instill them.

---

[14] *Fulfilling the Promise*, pp. 2, 18, 28, and 58.

Differentiation

When taking the necessary in-depth look at **Visible Learning** with the eye of an expert, we find not a mighty castle but a fragile house of cards that quickly falls apart.

... In summary, it is clear that John Hattie and his team have neither the knowledge nor the competencies required to conduct valid statistical analyses. No one should replicate this methodology because we must never accept pseudoscience. This is most unfortunate, since it is possible to do real science with data from hundreds of meta-analyses. [15]

---

[15] Bergeron, Pierre-Jérôme. "How to Engage in Pseudoscience with Real Data: A criticism of John Hattie's Arguments in Visible Learning, From the Perspective of a Statistician." *McGill Journal of Education.* 2017

3 Visible Learning

University of Melbourne professor John Hattie developed a theory he calls **Visible Learning**, and published his first book on the subject in 2009.[1] Based on how this book was regarded by my school district in 2012, you would have thought the skies had opened and rained down the panacea to all student achievement woes. Unlike *Fulfilling the Promise,* however, this book was not provided for us to read; our supervisors used it only to shape their philosophies and requirements.

According to one of Hattie's websites, "Visible Learning means an enhanced role for teachers as they become evaluators of their own teaching."[2] In a perfect educational world, teachers are not only training their students how to become metacognitive learners, they are also ***training themselves*** to become metacognitive teachers.

The essence of visible learning appeared to me (as it was explained by our principal) to be two-fold: first, teachers must teach in a way that makes it abundantly clear to students *why* they are learning *what* they are learning, and second, teachers should be using only the strategies that appear in the top ten or twenty in effectiveness, according to Hattie's research. Here is some clarification on that second point:

> According to Hattie's [2009] findings, visible learning occurs when teachers see learning through the eyes of students and help them become their own teachers. Hattie found that the ten most effective influences relating to student achievement are –
>
> 1. Student self-reporting grades (d = 1.44)
> 2. Formative evaluation (d = 0.9)
> 3. Teacher clarity (d = 0.75)

[1] Hattie, John. *Visible Learning*. Routledge, 2009
[2] Waack, Sebastian: https://visible-learning.org (About)

4. Reciprocal teaching (d = 0.74)
5. Feedback (d = 0.73)
6. Teacher-student relationships (d = 0.72)
7. Metacognitive strategies (d = 0.69)
8. Self-verbalization/ questioning (d = 0.64)
9. Teacher professional development (d = 0.62)
10. Problem-solving teaching (d = 0.61) [3]

This list is from 2009. Dr. Hattie's 2018 updated list includes the following top ten, different enough from the above list to make me wonder what research was involved in formulating it:

1. Collective teacher efficacy (d = 1.57)
2. Self-reported grades (d = 1.33)
3. Teacher estimates of achievement (d = 1.29)
4. Cognitive task analysis (d = 1.29)
5. Response to Intervention (RTI) (d = 1.29)
6. Piagetian programs (d = 1.28)
7. Jigsaw method (d = 1.20)
8. Conceptual change programs (d = 0.99)
9. Prior ability (d = 0.94)
10. Strategy to integrate with prior knowledge (d = 0.93) [4]

You can find the entire updated list at visible-learning.org (Hattie Rankings), but the first top ten list is the one we were given, and many of the strategies on it do seem more credible than Hattie's follow-up list. *Jigsaw method*, for instance, is the same technique used by Professional Development facilitators; you can see in chapter 4 (page 36) how seriously we teachers take *that*! (Do you think most students are any different?)[5]

What you may have noticed behind each item is "d = *number*". That's called the *effect size*, and it means the **effect of a strategy on student ability to learn**.

Hattie states that an effect size of d = 0.2 may be judged to have a **small effect**, d = 0.4 a **medium effect** and d = 0.6 a **large effect** on outcomes. He defines d = 0.4 to be the *hinge point*, an effect size at which an initiative can be said to be having a 'greater than average influence' on achievement...According to Hattie's work, teachers should be aiming for

[3] Wikipedia: *Visible Learning*. Accessed Feb 2022.
[4] Waack, Sebastian: www.visible-learning.org (Hattie Ranking)
[5] See chapter 23: Human Processes, in *Finishing School*.

achievement gains greater than d = 0.4 to be considered above average, and to be considered excellent they should demonstrate achievement gains for their students of d = 0.6 or higher. [6]

Way down on the list is Class Size, with an effect of 0.21 on student learning. That means that reducing class size has less effect on the ability to learn than Exercise/Relaxation, Problem-Based Learning or Using PowerPoint, all with an effect size of 0.26. In fact, Reducing Class Size is 186th on Hattie's list of 252 factors determining student achievement. Decreasing Disruptive Behaviors, incredibly, ranks 138th with an effect size of 0.34. My immediate question is, *How does he know this?* It certainly can't be from interviewing actual teachers in the field. And if he is relying on student data, how is that data culled?

Here are some of Hattie's other effect sizes, from least effective to greatest:

- Ability grouping for gifted learners = 0.30
- Manipulative materials in math = 0.30
- Classroom management = 0.35
- Motivation = 0.42, giving it an effect just above the hinge point mentioned on the previous page
- Early year interventions = 0.44 (programs like Head Start)
- Technology with elementary students = 0.44
- Small group learning = 0.47
- Note-taking = 0.50
- Teacher-student relationships = 0.52
- Prior achievement = 0.55
- Use of metacognitive strategies = 0.60, putting it in the high range of effects on learning, although probably not as high as Dr. Tomlinson would deem it.
- Direct instruction = 0.60
- Comprehensive instruction programs for teachers = 0.72. (Compare this with #9 on the first list. How do you know what qualifies as *'professional development'* and what would be considered *'instruction programs'*?)
- Interventions for students with learning needs = 0.77 (How is this different from #5 on the previous page: *Response to Intervention?*)
- Effort = 0.77

---

[6] Evans, Mark. "So…What Is the Evidence Base?"

- Classroom discussion = 0.82 [7]

Does anything on this list stand out as hard to believe? How about *prior achievement*, with an effect size of 0.55? That's not in the high range, like *prior ability*, #9 on page 24. (And how do you rate *prior ability* without looking at *prior achievement*, anyway?)

So what do these effect sizes mean?

They have to do with the achievement gains of a learner; the numbers correlate to yearly gains in learning. An effect size of 1.0 would equal a full school year of growth. How Hattie was able to test each strategy with validity, however, is something many experts have questioned.

When **Visible Learning** was introduced to our faculty in 2012, our principal, Rebecca, presented it as 'cutting-edge' and 'a game changer'. Her stance on it marked the beginning of our *"research-based"* era. Education elites insisted Dr. Hattie had approached learning from a mathematical angle and had years of data to support his theories, and Rebecca consistently pointed to that as a reason to adopt Hattie's strategies without question. Once I began researching Visible Learning for myself, however, I found numerous critiques, including this blog posted by a mathematician who calls himself Ollie Orange 2:

> Some of the statistical methods used by Hattie have been criticized. Hattie himself admitted that of every two statistics in Visible Learning, one was calculated incorrectly throughout the book. [8]

> John Hattie knows about this mistake but has chosen not to publicize it. This could mean that many teachers are still relying on it to instruct their teaching.
> No-one picked up on it for years, despite the fact the CLE [Common Language Effect size statistic] is meant to be a probability...So, who is checking John Hattie's work? [9]

And this blog by another mathematician:

> ... operating on the principle that anything that looks to be too good to be true probably is, I looked into Visible Learning to try to understand why it reports such large effect sizes ... And sure enough, Hattie is profoundly

---

[7] www.visible-learning.org (Hattie Rankings)
[8] OllieOrange2 Blog: "John Hattie Admits That Half of the Statistics in Visible Learning Are Wrong", Part One, Aug 2014
[9] OllieOrange2 Blog. Part Two, Sep 2014.

wrong. He is merely shoveling meta-analyses containing massive bias into meta-meta-analyses that reflect the same biases. [10]

Yet Hattie's preachings were presented to us as sacrosanct; not only were we to concentrate our instruction and activities on only those strategies appearing in his top ten or twenty list, but the suggestion that class size might be much more significant than Hattie's research indicated was a non-starter.

Then, we were shown videos of teachers using Hattie's techniques. As I watched these demonstrations, I found my hackles rising and my disbelief growing. Several departures from reality were on display:

- Each classroom had fewer than 15 students. And it's not that half the desks were empty. The room was set up for only that number of children, with plenty of space between work groups.
- Cameras were everywhere, much like a television studio. What kid is going to be off task with cameras present? (And even more interesting, how were these kids chosen in the first place? It seemed improbable that school-haters were recruited to be the actors.)
- The students shared exactly the ideas the teacher was trying to elicit, and everyone either participated or looked pensive throughout.

I wondered what might happen to those strategies with twice as many students and no cameras present. When I mentioned this to my sixth-grade colleagues, I was told to keep that to myself unless I enjoyed public humiliation. One colleague even tried to shame me: "*If our purpose is to serve our students, don't we owe it to them to follow the research presented to us?*"

I agree our purpose *is* to serve our students and give them full opportunities to learn. But to accept without question instructional theories that don't ring true from personal experience? And to ignore the implausibility of professionally produced videos? I found it hard to believe I was the only one noticing or taking issue with these things.

And now, on to the other part of Hattie's ideas: the 'visible' part.

Our principal explained that this means full transparency with our students. Our teaching should ensure that they are aware of not only *what* they are learning, but *why* they are learning it, and *how* it will benefit their lives. That type of messaging seems pretty obvious, doesn't it? We had been

---

[10] Robert Slavin's Blog. "John Hattie Is Wrong", 2018

teaching like that for years. But Rebecca informed us that, according to Dr. Hattie, we were doing it all wrong.

We were introduced to **Learning Goals**, **Learning Targets**, and **Success Criteria.** [11] All activities in our classrooms had to be labeled as such. We were to post them on a chart that had a prominent place at the front of our room. Every time we transitioned to a different lesson, we were to refer to the Learning Goal and then the daily Learning Target, using those exact terms.

The Learning Goals were to be drawn from the district's curriculum. They were the units of study, such as *Character Analysis in Short Stories*. We spent several hours during orientation week creating posters together so they would all have the same language. (Try to imagine *that* collaborative process.) Then we printed our posters and waited our turn at the laminator. And that was just for the first units of study in one subject. This had to be repeated for each unit in every subject, throughout the school year.

The Learning Target represented the day's lesson, and the Success Criteria was the daily assignment. It was not acceptable to write *'complete a worksheet'* but it *was* acceptable to write *'written practice to demonstrate learning'*. I pointed out that if I write *'worksheet* [along with its title]' on the board, it reminds students exactly what the "written practice" *is*. I was informed that the word *"worksheet"* sounds negative, so it could not be used. I wondered what synonyms for worksheet *could* be used and finally decided on *'think sheet'*, which *did* pass muster. I thought the term misleading, however, because it didn't give the impression that written work was required.

The large chart on the opposite page is an example of a correctly written learning chart. This chart, with its removable posters for learning goals and targets, had to be displayed every day. We put it on one section of our whiteboard so the posters could be easily attached and removed using magnetic strips.

We were instructed to post the Learning Goals and Learning Targets for every subject immediately in the morning, so students would have a picture of their entire day's study. The Success Criteria could be added after each lesson.

---

[11] John Hattie did not coin these terms; however, he popularized similar terms (learning intentions and success criteria) in his book *Visible Learning*.

	Learning Goals	Learning Targets	Success Criteria
Reading	Analyzing the parts of persuasive literature to understand its meaning.	Find evidence to support that you are reading persuasive writing.	Written practice to find evidence in 4 separate passages.
Writing	Writing persuasively requires ideas, organization, and voice.	Work in teams to help each other create an opinion statement about any of the ideas in your Think Journal.	Use a graphic organizer to brainstorm your evidence for the opinion statement you wrote.
Math	Using Ratios to Compare Quantities.	Examples of ratios occur in many ways. Practice in teams with ratio problems.	Use team collaboration to complete problems 15 – 25. Show your work and write justifications for 15, 17, and 21.
Social Studies	Regions: Grouping areas based on common traits or factors.	How do geographic factors impact the ways people live?	Complete a written activity to show what factors connect the Canadians who live on the western edge of their country.
Science	Atomic and molecular structure related to the properties of matter	Class Exploration: What makes an atom an atom?	Complete the Think Sheet on atomic structure with a partner.

The Learning Goals were the posters we had begun creating collaboratively during orientation week. They could remain posted for as long as a unit of study lasted.

The Learning Targets were also to be created collaboratively and changed according to what we were teaching that day. (We were all supposed to teach the same thing at the same time and to meet weekly to decide what that would be.)

The Success Criteria was handwritten and also had to be identical to what the other teachers on the team were assigning that day. On our team, this was rarely the case, but for some reason, our evaluator, Assistant Principal Gary Morris never called us out on it. That surprised me considering how much he seemed to dislike *me*. (More on that in chapter 10.)

Morris liked to wander the halls, glancing into classrooms to see what was going on. The first thing he would look for was this display. If it didn't appear to be filled out properly, an email was sure to follow.

Try to imagine being a kid looking at that chart. What stands out to you? It seems too crowded for *anything* to stand out. (And why on earth would we write *Success Criteria* instead of *Assignment*? This is the problem with education researchers telling us what to do. They have no practical experience with students, so they don't understand that phrases like "*success criteria*" elicit eye rolling and silly comments from adolescents.)

In contrast, here is what I posted prior to 2012:

Today's Writing Focus:	Assignment:
The importance of persuasion (Why and How is it useful?)	Persuasive Arguments Worksheet – Due by lunchtime.

This small chart was posted in the upper right corner of my whiteboard and changed with each subject lesson. As I transitioned, I transferred the assignment to my large assignment calendar posted by the door, instructing my students to add it to their own daily planner as well. We all did this on our sixth-grade team. We had found this practice quite effective at keeping our students focused on what was important and necessary. And prior to 2012, Rebecca had supported that.

But she and her two AP's became adamant in 2012 that Hattie and company were the holy grail of teaching. If we would only adjust our activities to include the practices he deemed valuable and follow his rules about transparency, our students would almost certainly respond positively.

What our principal didn't consider was the sustainability of using our prep time this way. There's only so much of it available in a teacher's day, and there's a lot of activity that must happen for that kid to look at this chart. Keeping up with it was time-consuming, and we were not supposed to do it on our own. We were instructed to meet regularly to decide, collectively, how to convert the curriculum standards into student-friendly language for our posters. Rebecca explained that this would make teaching a more reflective practice for us, *and* we would improve our ability to be both transparent with our students and metacognitive in our approach to delivering lessons.

Her mandate missed the mark, however. Poster-making became a going-through-the-motions activity. I could tell that Gary Morris didn't care about anything other than our compliance. If he did, he would have noticed that as the year wore on, the posters we put up on our charts were all different from each other: once we realized how this activity, which none of us thought was useful, was wasting our precious planning periods, we started making our posters independently and sharing what we had done with the others via email. We were already compelled to use our planning period once a week for other purposes, and when time ran out on that meeting, we postponed the poster discussion. After a few months, the requirement to talk about them just went by the wayside. I think it became a "Don't ask, don't tell" situation.

For some reason, and without explanation, this requirement lasted only for the school year 2012-13. When we arrived at our jobs the next August, nothing was said about it during orientation week, either that we needed to continue with the Hattie-style chart or that we should discontinue it. It was simply ignored. I was grateful that no one on the faculty was stupid enough to raise their hand in a meeting and ask, "What about the posters we made last year? Should we put those back up?"

I would see my stacks of posters neatly stored in my cupboard while looking for other teaching materials and shake my head in frustration. What was the purpose of having us do something so ridiculously time-consuming one year, only to abandon it without comment the next? Remember what I wrote on the first page of the *Foreword* about no strategy given much credence because teachers know that next year, something new will take its place? The fad called Visible Learning fits neatly into that box, and I often wondered, *Really, Rebecca...what's the bang for the buck?* [12]

2012 was a difficult year to teach. Sometimes, it felt like living in the Twilight Zone. We went from being able to use our planning periods for what *we* deemed necessary to being compelled to use many of them for redundant meetings and pointless activities. But even worse was the contradiction in the new messaging: simultaneous to being lectured about differentiation and finding out what works with each student, we were also harangued that uniformity is the key and that our strategies should mesh only with Hattie's lists.

I had doubts, because Dr. Tomlinson's and Dr. Hattie's theories did not appear to mesh *with one another*. The reaction I received when I mentioned that was not encouraging. For the previous seven years that Rebecca had been our principal, we had been able to discuss differing ideas in our professional development meetings. Beginning in August 2012, however, that was no

---

[12] You'll find another example of the pointlessness of this fad in chapter 7, "Data for Data's Sake".

longer the case, a situation that was made abundantly clear. Most teachers quietly accepted this, rather than bring up anything that would surely elicit condescension, if not outright disdain.

Research Visible Learning for yourself. You can start with visible-learning.org and visiblelearning.com to get the information that Hattie and his devotees want you to have. Following that, a search of 'Visible Learning Critiques' will net pages of material providing additional viewpoints. You'll also get some attempts to circumvent these critiques with rebuttals, such as this one posted to Corwin Connect: [13]

Clearing the Lens: Addressing the Criticisms of the VISIBLE LEARNING Research
June 22, 2018 / author: John Hattie
While the Visible Learning research has been spread all over the world and has been transforming schools and the way we teach, we can't be blind to the questions and criticisms that have also arisen from that spotlight.   I'd like to take this opportunity to address several of the criticisms we see more often below and, hopefully, clear the lens a bit...

Criticism #1. You keep adding more meta-analyses and more influences.
More needs to be added, because this is the nature of research—we continually question, query, replicate, and validate previous studies. It's exciting to us that researchers are still finding fascinating influences to investigate and thus they can be added to the database...

Dr. Hattie's response to the first criticism sounds very politician-y to me: vague and just a bit condescending. This article continues with responses to five more criticisms.   Class size is addressed in #4, though not very convincingly:

Qualitative studies [of things like class size] were not included because their findings can't be quantified in a manner to be used in a meta-analysis.

---

[13] Hattie, J. 2018.

I was hoping for a more comprehensive explanation for how decreasing class size is not considered significant for learning, especially since all the class sizes in Dr. Hattie's videos are so low.

The response to Criticism #5 *(Visible Learning seems to ignore the debate about...what subject matter is worth learning)* calls to mind the term '*doublespeak*' from page 1:

Visible Learning is not about the aims of education...but about understanding what works best in supporting student achievement.
However, one of the most exciting developments since Visible Learning was published is the emergence and growth of meta-synthesis of qualitative studies and I look forward to reading a synthesis of these studies that's similar to the Visible Learning work.

More doublespeak?

The goal was to increase difficulty across the board and aim for more uniformity across the country.
But soon after, Common Core faced some severe criticism from parents and teachers. They said the standards were overly challenging and questioned whether they encouraged an effective way of learning. [14]

---

[14] An, Susie and Adriana Cardona-Maguigad. "Common Core: Higher Expectations, Flat Results", 2019.

4 The Common Core Conundrum

Later in the fall of 2012, we teachers were introduced to the Common Core standards. Well, not exactly the standards, but a way to implement the rigor the standards represent. The state of Colorado had adopted the CC standards in 2010, but that information (or the specific standards) was not shared with teachers. (At least not in my school.)

At our first training, we were handed a thin book and told that our professional development would center around it for the year. We heard the words *rigor* and *metacognition* numerous times in those sessions. Common Core asserts that *all students benefit from a sense of rigor*. What it does not make clear without intense further study is that this idea of rigor means pushing children faster than their developmental stage might allow for.

The book we were given touts itself as being written for *"educators who already have a strong grasp on the Common Core and are eager to do something about it."* [1] None of us knew anything about Common Core prior to being given this book as a model for designing our instruction. Imagine our surprise upon reading that sentence that appears on page one.

As I read the material, it appeared to me that it was written for working with highly motivated and possibly advanced learners, but it was presented by our supervisors as the recipe for success with *all* students, regardless of cognitive development or motivation. If we would just implement the strategies with fidelity, all struggles in learning would fade away. [2] How realistic does that seem? This type of lecturing is a major reason that

---

[1] Silver, Dewing, and Perini: *The Core Six: Essential Strategies for Achieving Excellence with the Common Core*, p. 1.
[2] The lecturing surrounding this book sounded remarkably similar to the lecturing we were given a few weeks earlier regarding Hattie's Visible Learning.

professional development, delivered *en masse* to a large faculty, is met with disfavor by the participants.

Gary Morris, our new PD guru, spear-headed our study.

We were put into groups to discuss each chapter. This is a common modern tactic of Professional Development: mix the faculty into groups and assign each a task. During discussion, they write their findings on chart paper. After a half hour or more, the groups share out with the larger group. This exercise is utter drudgery, as all the "noticings" begin to sound alike. Those teachers who are either new or trying to butter-up admin are overly eager and chirpy. Those who consider it a waste of time are multi-tasking in their lap and barely make eye contact when spoken to.

At one point during my group's discussion, Gary Morris approached our table to listen.

I was addressing seventh-grade colleague Eileen, who was arguing that the book didn't say students must be able to engage in writing about their learning.

"Right here," I pointed out, "on page 51, it says that *'writing is the skill most directly related to improved scores in reading, social studies, science, and even mathematics'*." [3] What do you think that means?"

Maureen said, "TerryLynn makes a good point. It does say that, Eileen."

"How does that work in math?" Paige from fourth grade wanted to know, and I turned a few pages of the book, looking for examples.

"It doesn't address math specifically," I told her. "But it does say that when a student writes, it gives the teacher insight into their thought process so they can provide meaningful feedback."

"So does talking to them," George had inserted dryly.

"So," Paige continued, "it's not enough for a student to correctly use the algorithm for solving a problem. He must express in words why he set it up the way he did? In fourth grade?"

My thought at that moment was that the child who does not write well but does have a talent for math suddenly finds himself a failure in a subject he thought was his strong suit.

"Is there a problem?" Gary Morris had asked, stopping at the end of our table.

Maureen responded neutrally, "We're making our observations about what the authors say about metacognitive writing."

"It sounds like you all don't approve of the strategy," Morris said.

---

[3] Silver, Dewing, and Perini: *The Core Six,* p. 51.

Paige had defended herself. "I'm having trouble with the idea that *writing* about math is the only way to learn it," she said, and the rest of us waited.

"Studies show," Morris told us, "that in today's world, students must be able to express their reasoning." Paige nodded a little. "Otherwise, they're just mindlessly performing tasks. We want them to have reasoning abilities and logic on their side."

Well, of course, I had thought. *But do you really think this strategy is going to fix a reluctant student's struggles? And why is it the only way to approach learning?*

"What studies?" George asked.

Morris did not smile as he replied, "Multiple studies conducted by various accredited organizations."

When none of us responded to that, Morris continued. "The sooner you get on board with the new way of thinking and teaching, the better off all of you will be."

After he walked away, Maureen said, "Well, shall we all get on board and finish this up?"

What is Common Core?

Common Core is a set of standards that pushes kids faster than previously, in their elementary education particularly.

It flies in the face of individualized instruction, which promotes meeting a child where his developmental stage indicates he is ready. It also contradicts the philosophy of a democratic society: the idea that people get to choose their own path in life. Common Core dictates advanced concepts as early as kindergarten, when students are expected to understand place value in a base ten system, and third grade, when students begin their foray into multiplication, division, fractions, and algebraic expressions, and write analyses of character development in books like *Charlotte's Web*. It appears to presume that all students are gifted and should be prepped for graduate school starting at a young age.

In my research for this book, I found the following statement, written by Susi An and Adriana Cardona-Maguigad for NPR station WBEZ in Chicago: "Common Core is not a curriculum, rather it's a set of detailed expectations for what content and skills students should master at each grade level. The goal is to dig deep into topics rather than scratch the surface on a broad range of content."[4]

Isn't that what a curriculum is? The content and skills students should master at each grade level? Common Core *does* provide that set of skills from which everything else is derived: textbooks, tests, and individual school district curricula. You can see it on their own website, CoreStandards.org.

And yes, the goal is to dig deep into topics. In fifth grade, for instance, math students are expected to *"solve real world problems involving multiplication of fractions and mixed numbers...by using visual fraction models or equations to represent the problem."* [5] A current fifth grade math workbook contains the following problem, inspired by this expectation:

> Josie sold 3/7 of all the ears of corn she brought to the market in the morning and 2/3 of the remaining ears of corn in the afternoon. She sold 255 ears of corn in all. She donated the leftover ears of corn to the food bank. How many ears of corn did she donate to the food bank? [6]

If your fifth grader is getting questions like this in his school workbook, you know he is also getting questions like this on your state's standardized test. When you receive a report that his proficiency level on that test is mid-range or low, how seriously are you going to take the results? Even elementary school teachers, for the most part, cannot answer this question without guidance from the teacher's manual.

This material, prior to 2010, was first taught in middle school, when teachers begin to specialize in a single subject, like math. Not in elementary school. Students are now taught equivalent fractions in third grade (which means GCF and LCM) [7] and decimal/fraction comparisons in fourth. By sixth grade, students should be solving problems like this: [8]

> Create a story context for (2/3) ÷ (3/4) and use a visual fraction model to show the quotient; use the relationship between multiplication and division to explain that (2/3) ÷ (3/4) = 8/9 because 3/4 of 8/9 is 2/3. [9]

A story context means students write their own word problem. Yes, this is rigor. No, it should not be considered typical sixth grade material.

[4] Cardona-Maguigad and An: "Common Core: Higher Expectations, Flat Results", 2019.
[5] *Common Core, Grade 5 Math*: https://corestandards.org/wp-content/uploads/2023/09/Math_Standards1.pdf, p. 36.
[6] *Dimensions Math Workbook 5A*, p. 129.
[7] GCF: Greatest Common Factor; LCM: Least Common Multiple. Prior to Common Core, this was taught to advanced 5th graders and all 6th graders in my school.
[8] *Common Core State Standards Initiative* http://www.corestandards.org/Math/Content/6/NS/
[9] *Common Core, Grade 6 Math*: http://www.corestandards.org/Math/Content/6/NS/

It is a major leap to require students to *write their own "story context"* from the information presented in that problem. (And the only way the problem makes sense at all is if reciprocal fractions make sense to the student.) To be sure, some students *will* demonstrate readiness for this, and they should be placed in classes with other learners of a similar ilk. But to require all sixth graders to understand and demonstrate mastery of fractions and their reciprocals to the extent that they could complete the problem on the previous page is unrealistic and sets many students up for failure.

A major fall-out from instituting these advanced standards across the board is that many students are resisting the push toward faster and more in-depth learning.

Nothing is riding on their engagement in the program, so they opt out because it is easier than pushing themselves beyond their comfort level. Most students don't care whether they do well on the state tests that were developed using the core standards. They are not compelled to care.

Teachers, however, *do* obsess over these tests because *they* must. It has become an ongoing conundrum in education: how to make students *want* to learn material that is either too difficult *for* them or uninteresting *to* them. Telling a child that he needs to know material he is not ready to learn leads to dismal results. Instead, we should observe the natural development of children in grades K-5 and sort them into the groups (classes) that will benefit them the most. Some will land in those Common Core classes because they are advanced thinkers. Others will not. That is the way things work developmentally.

Teaching all students at a similar age the same advanced material regardless of their readiness and holding them all accountable for learning objectives that are not doable for some frustrates everyone in the program.

If we are patient, and we offer supports and differentiated instruction, students will understand the material when *they* are ready to understand it. There is also the aspect of effort to consider. How much is a student *willing* to push himself? When students are counseled about the choices they are making and then placed in classes according to those choices, their education will mean more to them.

This is why there should be leveled classes all along the path toward high school graduation and diligent adults watching for student readiness.

Common Core proponents claim their program is for *College and Career Readiness*. The standards requiring all students to write and graph linear, quadratic, and exponential functions belie that. (I urge you to explore the Math Standards at CoreStandards.org for a full picture of the math prowess we are now requiring from all high school students.[10]) Career readiness cannot be neatly defined using one brush stroke. High schoolers are not stupid; just because we insist on a certain path for them, regardless of their dreams or abilities, doesn't mean they're going to buy into our plan. What it means is that they will gradually put less and less stock in what the power structure says, even to their own detriment. Pushing students toward a goal that means little to *them* is futile.

Middle school programs should begin the process of counseling students to determine what they imagine their path in life will be and then tracking kids toward those goals through placement in realistic (and appropriately challenging) classes that meet their needs. If we have already begun ability grouping in elementary school, this will be even more seamless.

Insisting that all students travel an advanced path through high school graduation encourages cynicism in our young people and chaos for them as they contemplate their future.

Why Common Core?

According to Catherine Gewertz, writing for **Education Week**, Common Core was developed as a response to the push to create shared standards, nationwide:

> The push to create shared standards took shape in part because of a key failing of the standards movement that swept the country in the 1990s. States began writing their own standards after the 1983 report "A Nation at Risk" warned of a "rising tide of mediocrity" in American schools. But the **quality of those academic expectations varied from state to state.** And even when the federal No Child Left Behind Act (signed into law in 2001) required states to test students' mastery of those standards annually, and face consequences for students' poor performance, some states set far higher proficiency goals than others.
>
> State leaders also cited high college-remediation rates as evidence that more-rigorous, shared standards were needed. When **1 in 5 college**

---

[10] https://corestandards.org/ , pp. 57-83.

students has skills too weak for credit-bearing coursework, they argued, the K-12 system is falling short in preparing young people for the postsecondary work that leads to good jobs. Surveys of employers, too, showed widespread dissatisfaction with the literacy and math skills of young job applicants.

The idea, then, was to "raise the bar" for all students to create better college and work outcomes and establish a common bar by which all students could be measured [11]

This post on *Quora.com* offers an additional viewpoint:

> I've been to several professional development classes about Common Core, including one lecture given by one of the people who helped come up with the CC standards. I know why they did it. They started at the top and worked backwards. They asked colleges what new students should know on day one, then figured out where those students should be in 12th grade, 11th grade, etc. [12]

These excerpts indicate that the push for national rigorous standards originated at the university level: freshmen were arriving on campus without the requisite skills for success. **What is not clear is whether this phenomenon was a curriculum problem or a deployment issue.** In other words, is it because students were not being taught useful material? Or is it that the students were not mastering what they had been taught? Perhaps, even, they were not matched with the proper classes in high school.

The more one probes the idea of college students arriving at freshman year unprepared academically, the more one is likely to associate the problem with *what students have been taught.* (Especially if that person has not been present to see how implementation of instruction is handled.) It is no wonder a group of self-proclaimed experts thought they could fix things by focusing only on *that* and how to make it more rigorous.

But there's more to learning than the *what* and the *how.* There's also the *who*, which starts with the teachers. In the years prior to Common Core, elementary teachers were largely able to teach what they wanted and ignore the rest. Take writing instruction, for instance. It is not feasible to write effectively without some knowledge of grammar and syntax, yet that area of learning is not popular with a lot of K-5 teachers. When I was substituting prior to securing my Colorado teaching job, I noticed that very few teachers

---

[11] Gewertz, Catherine. "The Common Core Explained", 2015.
[12] Bates, Matthew. "Why Do So Many People Hate Common Core?", 2017.

I substituted for were teaching grammar or sentence structure. But language arts skills are cumulative: they must be introduced early and expanded upon every year after. Once a child reaches middle school without this foundational knowledge, the probability of developing adequate writing skills is low.

If we examine middle school and high school teaching, will we find a similar situation, where teachers were able to pick and choose what parts of the curriculum they wished to address?

So I ask again:

Is it a curriculum problem or a deployment issue?

It appears that the push to improve the quality of K-12 education followed the adage of *'throwing the baby out with the bathwater'*. Instead of addressing what was going awry about student acquisition of skills, a group of experts decided to drain the tub and start over. The new soapy mess that now engulfs education ignores multiple factors of success in learning, not the least of which is student readiness.

Obviously, rigor is a good and necessary ingredient in education. Going along with that, however, is **how the learner responds to the rigor**. Based on nationally dismal test scores, I'd say there's a disconnect that this redesigned curriculum failed to fix.

If you have not yet done so, explore The Common Core State Standards Initiative, available at CoreStandards.org. You'll see what I mentioned about kindergarten math: the standards include understanding single numbers as digits only. These digits receive their value from the place they occupy in a multi-digit number. Kindergarteners are five years old. Sure, they can be instructed to group items into tens to begin an understanding of the base ten system. But place value itself is an abstract notion. Children typically do not begin abstract thinking as kindergartners. Assuming that every child is capable of it subtly encourages social-emotional issues.

Some of those children *will* jump ahead in their understanding. This is when the sorting of learners should begin. Everyone's needs can then be met more effectively. Currently, however, all learners are kept together in heterogeneous groups, discouraging effective differentiation and acceleration. (Remember what I wrote on page 18 about everyone moving at the pace of the slowest member.)

Many teachers I know purchase workbooks that are a grade level *under* the grade they are teaching. This is because the current trend for education publishers is to market their products for Common Core instruction. That's a red flag that means the material will be too advanced for many of one's students. The savvy teacher keeps workbooks of several levels on hand so she can pull from any of them based on the displayed aptitude of her students.

If you go onto Amazon and look at the free samples available for the *Spectrum* series of reading workbooks, for instance, you will see that the reading level of a third-grade workbook appears to be geared more toward students in fourth or even fifth grade. And it's not just the reading level; it's the types of questions that are posed. One question after a short story about children making drawings on a sidewalk asks, *"Why is the story titled 'Wishes on the Sidewalk'?"* [13] This question requires students to interpret the meaning behind the dialogue and the setting. With students who understand that it has no one right answer, it can elicit all sorts of creative brain power. For those who don't, however, it usually elicits a very literal response along the lines of this: *"Because it's hot and they wish they had some ice cream?"*

The education elite tell us to go ahead and give our learners questions like this, anyway. Even if they aren't ready for it now, eventually, they will be. That's like saying, "Go ahead and teach Driver's Ed. to second graders. Eventually, they'll find it useful." The only practical use for this third-grade question is helping us understand how to sort our learners for maximum reading comprehension development.

It's time we think about Common Core from the students' perspective. Their self-confidence surely must suffer when they *repeatedly* encounter questions they *know* they are expected to understand but don't. They've been harangued for years, even prior to COVID, that they do not measure up. For many of them, it must seem impossible to ever reach their *proper* grade level.

And what happens to their morale when they see that their instruction comes from workbooks that are *below* their supposed grade level? It is a sad fact that many, many teachers are delivering their main reading and math instruction from supplemental materials rather than the grade-level textbook series they have been provided by their district because they know the Common Core textbooks do not meet their students' needs. Those who *are* teaching from the grade level textbooks (usually because their principal

---

[13] *Spectrum Reading Grade 3*, p. 113. Carson-Dellosa Education, 2015.

insists on it) find themselves continually modeling for their students how to do *everything*. Very little independent work occurs, particularly in math. This is one reason students have so much trouble when they sit down to take a solo test, such as what you'll see in the next chapter.

The Final Analysis

The Common Core philosophy appears to be that every child is capable of functioning at the far-right of the cognitive bell-curve, and we know that cannot possibly be true. Children fall all along that curve, based on their innate intellect and developmental stage. Effective instruction will no doubt improve a child's chances of learning, but what is also needed is effort from the child *himself*.

And therein lies the problem:

Students are not held accountable for the effort they put toward learning. There are no ramifications for their disengagement, and that disengagement is the genesis of the problem.

How do we get students to *want* to better themselves? That is the nut that must be cracked. In my experience as a teacher, I have found that sparking a child's curiosity is key to encouraging the motivation to learn. Common Core's strategy appears to be browbeating our students into submission. That has led to a massive pushback, something that should be evident when you look at test scores.

Additionally, the very things that teachers use to try to spark this curiosity (online learning and videos) have also been working *against* helping students develop the work ethic necessary to learn deeply: for almost their whole life, they've been handed Smart devices whenever they felt fussy or bored.

So just how useful is Common Core, a program that pushes learners to the limit of their endurance, with students who have been raised on soft expectations?

The trouble with our elementary schools is that there is no incentive to achieve. The cure for that is not in instituting advanced, across the board standards that ignore cognitive development. It is in **setting the expectation that students will work hard at learning**... and backing that up with appropriate class placements.

I'll leave you with one final thought about Common Core standards and the tests that measure them: they have been around for more than a decade. If they made sense, wouldn't we see results that show mastery more often than not? After all, if you begin in kindergarten to teach the standards and follow the curricula with fidelity year after year (as teachers assure us through their documentation they are doing), the majority of sixth graders *should* be able to pass the Common Core tests. However, according to Colorado's reporting of its 2025 CMAS scores, **only 23% of sixth graders[14] met or exceeded proficiency expectations in Math.**[15]   For reading (ELA), the percentage is significantly higher, but still below 40%, nothing to be proud of. During the COVID years of 2020 and 2021, much of the state testing was suspended, as you can see from the chart below. Even pre-COVID results, however, do not reassure that Common Core is a reasonable or realistic set of expectations:[16]

Year	6th grade Percentage of students **achieving at or above** proficiency on state test		3rd grade Percentage of students **achieving at or above** proficiency on state test	
2025	23% Math	37% ELA	36% Math	37% ELA
2024	29% Math	44% ELA	42% Math	42% ELA
2023	28% Math	43% ELA	40% Math	40% ELA
2022	26% Math	43% ELA	40% Math	41% ELA
2021	24% Math	-------------	---------------	
2020	---------------		---------------	
2019	30% Math	44% ELA	41% Math	41% ELA
2018	30% Math	43% ELA	39% Math	41% ELA
2017	31% Math	41% ELA	40% Math	40% ELA
2016	31% Math	38% ELA	39% Math	38% ELA

Visit SchoolMattersFoundation.org/testing for a sample of the test questions we are using to assess grade level proficiency.

---

[14] Non-Gifted & Talented students only. GT students tested at 87% proficient or above for math. A blended statistic is not available at www.CDE.state.co.us.
[15] CMAS: Colorado Measures of Academic Success, the successor to TCAP. CMAS is a test that includes questions developed by Colorado and PARCC (New Meridian). Non-GT students only in this cohort. GT cohort tested at 87% proficient or above for math.
[16] CMAS Test Results: https://www.cde.state.co.us/assessment/2023 and https://www.cde.state.co.us/assessment/cmas-dataandresults-2025

Standardized testing destroys teaching's true purpose. Teachers no longer teach so students learn the material, but so that students pass and make themselves look good. They become robots of the education system. [17]

---

[17] Marissa Engman in *The World*: "Standardized Testing is Ineffective". 19 Mar 2018. https://theworldlink.com/opinion/

5 Testing, Part One

It is routine in most schools to provide periodic assessments that we call 'formative'. This means the test gives us "actionable" data: we can use it to determine how to steer that child's individualized instruction.

All of the popular testing platforms in this country have now been adapted to test the Common Core standards. Here is an example of a fourth-grade math question from NWEA's MAP Growth test: [1]

MAP Math Sample Question 1

The following question tests a student's problem-solving skills. It corresponds to an RIT score of 201-210, which is an average fourth grade score.

A snail takes one and a half days to travel one mile.
How long would it take a snail to travel two miles?

Select all the correct answers.

      a.   36 hours
      b.   72 hours
      c.   3 days
      d.   4 days
      e.   4.5 days [2]

To answer this correctly, the student needs to be able to add improper fractions ($1\frac{1}{2} + 1\frac{1}{2}$), cross reference his calculation with the wording in the

---

[1] NWEA: *Northwest Evaluation Association*, a not-for-profit group that has created assessments for K-12 learning for more than 40 years, according to its website: www.nwea.org/. MAP: Measures of Academic Progress, an aptitude test of the NWEA that adapts to the student's achievement level as he tests.

[2] MAP Growth sample question taken from the website Test Prep Online

problem ("days") and convert the days to hours to select both answers that are correct. This is after interpreting the problem accurately in the first place (e.g. "Select all the correct answers."). A fourth grader is nine or ten years old. Try to imagine any ten-year-old you know sticking with this problem with fidelity. (Especially if he doesn't care about it.)

This math sample question was taken from **Test Prep Online**, a commercial website designed to give parents paid access to testing practice for at least 20 tests given to school age children and an additional 10 tests for admission to college, as listed on its Home Page.

The only motivation provided to the student for taking this test is that we (the school) need to know what he is ready to learn next. We implore the children to take the test seriously throughout the 40 or so questions on it.

I cannot imagine any instance in which one would take seriously an assessment whose outcome admittedly did nothing for *them*. And that *is* the case with these tests. Nothing will happen with the child's school program, regardless of his skill acquisition.

In addition to periodic formative assessments, students are given the state's summative assessment, usually in March or April each school year. My former state of Colorado used CSAP (Colorado Student Assessment Program) from 1997 to 2011 and then TCAP (Transitional Colorado Assessment Program) until 2015, when it implemented CMAS (Colorado Measures of Academic Success)[3] a PARCC-inspired battery of assessments in ELA and Math. (Certain students also test in science and social studies.) PARCC creates assessments designed to measure a child's *College and Career Readiness*, a current buzz phrase in education. [4]

On the next few pages, you see a fourth grade PARCC released item in math from 2019. I found it online as a pdf from a search of PARCC released items. [5]

For the student to respond correctly, he needs to be able to read and accurately interpret all its parts, as well as type his responses meaningfully into text boxes.

These questions are for fourth grade. See how well *you* do.

---

[3] Colorado Department of Education: CSAP/TCAP
[4] PARCC: *The Partnership for Assessment of Readiness for College and Careers* is a consortium of states that collaboratively developed a common set of assessments to measure student achievement and preparedness for college and careers.
[5] Go Test Prep: 2019-Math-Grade-4-Released-Items.pdf All the test items shared in this chapter are available as free previews on the sites I culled from.

Marcy and her friends recorded how long it took each of them to read the same book. Their results are shown in the table:

Book Reading

Name	Number of Minutes
Marcy	35
Tom	37
Jennifer	28
Darnel	31

Part A

Marcy wants to record the data on a bar graph. Which bar graph correctly shows the length of time each student read?

A.

Book Reading

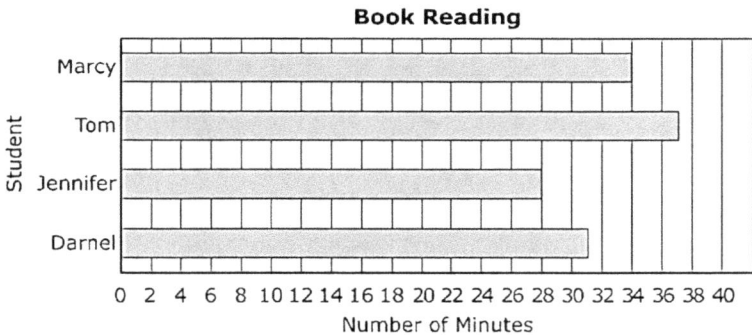

B.

Book Reading

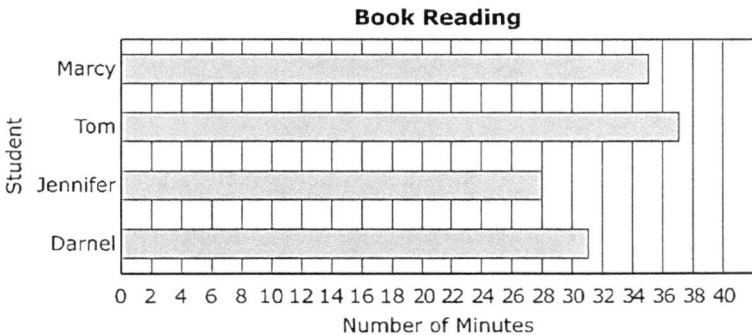

C.

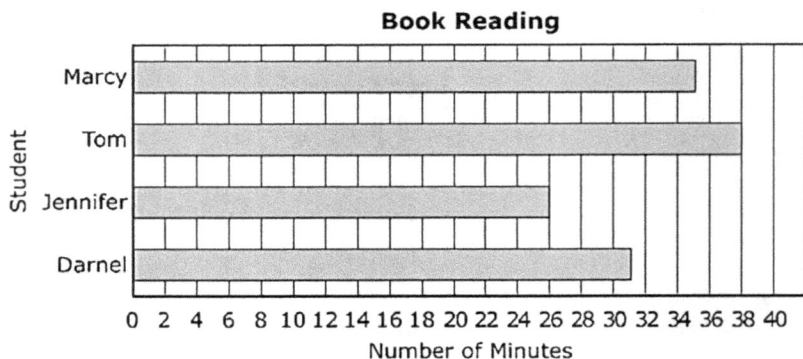

D.

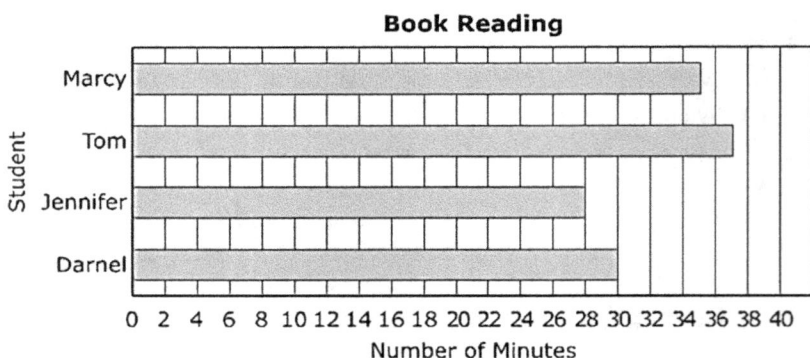

Part B

Explain how Marcy selected where the ends of the bars for Tom and Darnell should be. Enter your explanation in the space provided:

Part C

How many more minutes did Marcy and Tom read together than Jennifer and Darnell read together?

Show the work you used to find out how many more minutes it took Marcy and Tom to read the book than it did for Jennifer and Darnell to read the book.

Enter your answer and your work in the space provided:

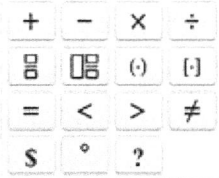

Did you notice the question posed in Part B? Do *you* understand what this question is getting at? I do, but it took me about 20 seconds. How long do you think the average ten-year-old is going to persist? And there's something else to consider: if the child chooses answer *C* or *D* for Part A, the question posed in Part B will not make sense. And he can't ask his teacher, even for clarification of what is being asked.

Now look again at Part C above. In order to "show work", the student must use the symbols next to the text box. So he has to type a number, look for a symbol, type another number, look for another symbol, etc, etc, etc. Again...how long do you think a kid will persist with this process? And, of course, there is no asking his teacher for clarification. The fact is, **the way we test our students directly contradicts how researchers encourage us to teach them** for optimum learning and retention of material.

On that same fourth grade test, here is the set-up for a geometry problem:

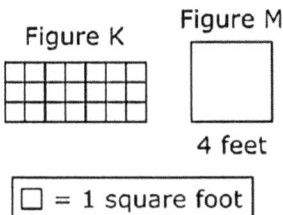

Figure K is covered with square tiles each measuring 1 foot square. There are no gaps or overlaps in the tiles. Figure M is a square with side lengths of 4 feet.

Students use this information to solve Parts A and B below:

Part A

Joan said the area of Figure K is found by adding 3 + 7 + 3 + 7, so the area is 20 square feet. Joan made a mistake in her reasoning.

Explain the mistake Joan made. Find the correct area for Figure K.

Enter your explanation and your answer in the space provided:

▾ Math symbols

+	−	×	÷
吕	口吕	(·)	[·]
=	<	>	≠
$	°	?	

Part B

Figures K and M are pushed together to form a larger figure. There are no gaps or overlaps of the two figures. To find the area of the larger figure, Andy multiplied the area of Figure K by the area of Figure M. Andy is incorrect in his reasoning.

- Explain the steps Andy should take to find the area of the larger figure.
- What is the area, in square feet, of the larger figure?
- Show your work or explain your answers.

Enter your explanation, your answer, and your work or explanation in the space provided:

▾ Math symbols

+	−	×	÷
吕	口吕	(·)	[·]
=	<	>	≠
$	°	?	

The questions in Parts A and B address Common Core's insistence on students thinking deeply, beyond simply understanding how to calculate area. However, if the student has trouble typing his mathematical reasoning in the text boxes, he does not get full credit, even if he shows a correct calculation. Now look at Part B again: as you wade through the setup and requirements, remember that the student reading this is a fourth grader. Did *you* give up part way through? What do you think the kid is going to do...?[6]

Here is an example of a useful math question:

Select each statement that can be represented by the equation 11 x 32 = 352. Select the two correct statements:

- ☐ A. 352 is 32 more than 11.
- ☐ B. 352 is 32 times as many as 11.
- ☐ C. 352 equals 11 times as many as 32.
- ☐ D. 352 is 11 more than 32.
- ☐ E. 352 multiplied by 11 is the same as 32.

Why is it useful? A correct response can help us separate the divergent thinkers from those who are not. This should be considered an important distinction in effective differentiation.

Let's turn our focus now to reading. Here is a fourth-grade item from a practice test from the same website (Go Test Prep). See what you think about the complexity of this article and the questions embedded within:

Reading Practice Test – Grade 4 (Reading Comprehension)
FOR ALL QUESTIONS: READ EACH PASSAGE. THEN ANSWER EACH QUESTION CAREFULLY BY CHOOSING THE BEST ANSWER.

Happiness may be the primary goal of human existence. Philosophers have wrestled with the concept of happiness. Legislators create laws to support citizens' rights to pursue happiness. Television, radio, and print advertisers assure consumers that various products will guarantee happiness. Interestingly, people have a tendency to believe they are happier than their neighbors, and they are optimistic about their happiness in the future. Most people

---

[6] See more examples of math problems for 4th and 5th graders at www.schoolmattersfoundation.org/testing.

assume that they will be happier a decade from now than they are today.

Clearly, everyone from writers and philosophers to legislators and the average person on the street thinks a great deal about happiness. What makes happiness so important to human existence?

Why Be Happy?

Not only does happiness feel good, but it appears to provide a variety of psychological and physical benefits. Happiness plays a significant role in enhancing good health, strengthening the immune system, promoting longevity, improving productivity and performance, and increasing resilience. Happy people work hard, play hard, have an active social life (and a social conscience), experience good health, and live longer. A happy person lives an average of nine years longer than a miserable one.

1. In the section **Why Be Happy**?, why does the author include parentheses around "and a social conscience"?
    a.   to point out that social conscience leads to good health
    b.   to emphasize the importance of playing and working hard
    c.   to point out that having a social conscience can promote longevity
    d.   to emphasize the importance of social conscience as a part of an active social life

The Opposite of Happiness

When studying happiness, it makes sense that its opposite condition would also be a topic of examination. Scientists have observed that there are two unfortunate life events that induce profound unhappiness, perhaps over the course of many years: the loss of a spouse and the loss of a job.

2. What change occurs as a result of adding the prefix *un–* to fortunate in the above paragraph?
    a.   the word becomes more intense
    b.   the word becomes less intense
    c.   the word takes on the opposite meaning
    d.   the word takes on a different part of speech

What Causes Happiness?

However, good news abounds in the study of happiness. Fortunately, humans experience happiness from a wide range of stimuli, from traveling to an exotic destination to redecorating one's home or from winning a game of soccer to eating a delicious meal. Simply watching a favorite television show or laughing at a funny joke can boost a depressed mood. While the happiness produced by such experiences tends to be short lived, certain conditions do promote a more long-lasting and durable state of happiness as a lifestyle: a wide social network, believing in a meaningful reason for one's existence, and establishing goals and working to achieve them.

3. Which statement summarizes the heading **What Causes Happiness**?
   a. A wide social network is the key to happiness.
   b. Laughing at funny jokes helps to lift a gloomy mood.
   c. Scientists conclude that good news leads to long-lasting happiness.
   d. Both short- and long-term happiness are caused by a variety of experiences.

With a Little Help from My Friends

Surprisingly, income is not a primary factor in determining a person's level of happiness once the basic needs of food, clothing, and shelter have been met. More important is one's social network. Being socially active may be more effective in increasing one's immunity to illness than a vaccine. Misery may love company, but so does happiness, and having close friends and family is vital to one's overall level of happiness. (If friends and family are crucial, so is a loving partner. Research suggests that being married increases one's potential for happiness.) Even sharing one's home with an animal companion can make a person happier.

4. In the section **With a Little Help from My Friends**, why does the author use the phrase "misery may love company"?
   a. to convince people that pets are better company than a loving partner
   b. to encourage people to find mates for their friends who are unhappy
   c. to point out that people will be happier with positive relationships
   d. to recommend that people try to influence negative people in a positive way

Why Am I Here?

Scientists report that believing in some kind of meaning for one's life is necessary to living a happy life. This may be a religion, a code of ethics, a particular value system, a philosophy, or any other reason for being that lifts people out of the mundane routine of daily existence and gives their life meaning beyond a weekly paycheck.

The Habit of Happiness

Happiness is not an innate characteristic but may actually be developed as a habit. Scientists suggest that incorporating new habits and practices can go a long way in increasing one's state of happiness. While people generally do not transform their basic temperaments, people can learn to become happier by participating in a variety of activities, including socializing, watching funny movies or reading funny books, keeping a gratitude journal (writing a daily list of three to five things for which one is grateful), involving oneself in pleasurable activities, such as sports, hobbies, or the arts, focusing on positive outcomes, and performing acts of kindness for others. Apparently, doing something to make someone else happy will make you happy, too.

5. What is one assumption the author makes about attaining happiness?
    a.   Some people find comfort in mundane routines
    b.   A person needs a social network to attain happiness.
    c.   Reading and writing about your problems will produce happiness.
    d.   Convincing negative people to become positive is a life goal.

6. In the section **The Habit of Happiness**, what does the word *innate* mean?
    a.   natural and existing
    b.   incomplete and building
    c.   absent and unfamiliar
    d.   learned and habitual

7. Which statement is an opinion?
    a.   Happiness is not a physical characteristic.
    b.   Legislators create laws to support happiness.
    c.   Happiness may be the primary goal of human existence.
    d.   Advertisers use happiness to promote their products.[7]

---

[7] https://gotestprep.com/reading-practice-test-4/

This is what *any* fourth grader should be able to comprehend three-quarters through his school year, according to Common Core. At least the questions are interspersed throughout the reading passage. That helps a child maintain focus. Still, any ten-year-old taking this test needs great powers of perseverance to stick with it. He also needs a broad vocabulary and an understanding of complex sentence structure. There is no way this is fourth grade material. If a child can understand this article and answer all or most of the questions, he is a gifted reader. That is unusual, not common. Yet we use reading selections like this to tell us whether children are functioning *on* grade level.

The standardized tests we give our children are long and arduous. After completing a session (typically there are five for the PARCC), students are usually drained for the rest of their school day. We show videos for enrichment and provide "fun" activities to counteract that brain depletion.

Look for yourself at the questions on these standardized assessments. Released items are readily available online through different search queries. Here is what I used:

Released PARCC items

Sample MAP questions

Tell me you would try your hardest if you were a kid, knowing the outcome of the test meant nothing to you. You wouldn't even see what you missed on it so you could learn something from your mistakes. Your teacher doesn't know, either. All she gets is a spreadsheet showing what category your deficits lie in.

The report you get as a parent tells you what *Level of Success* your child has reached for his grade level, with Level Five being the highest. If your child's report labels him at Level Three, you might be tempted to believe he is significantly behind in his learning, when his development might actually be typical and reasonable.

Parents and teachers should approach testing results with a wary eye. Not only do they report on advanced standards, they do not realistically account for tester motivation.

Formative assessments like MAP Growth theoretically provide teachers a plethora of information about where effective instruction should be placed. Still, that data is only useful if teachers can be assured students shared whey actually do know rather than skipping questions they don't feel like struggling with or clicking any answer just to be done with it. (See chapter 15, page 170, for more on this topic.)

Teachers spend *hours* of instructional time prepping students for their yearly standardized test, to the exclusion of the regular curriculum, using websites that are designed solely for that purpose.

Testing and test preparation are a big industry in this country: the online test prep company I've cited throughout this chapter does not exist out of a sense of philanthropy. The billions poured into creating tests and procuring results that can then be analyzed endlessly is mind-blowing.

If you are a parent, it is well worth your while to explore what is available, and read the advice offered to you by people who have a lot of skin in the game:

> Test Prep Online offers this advice to parents:
>
> Practice, practice, and more practice. The PARCC assesses skill and knowledge as well as reasoning and understanding. The techniques and thinking processes assessed by the PARCC are not only relevant for your child's current grade, but also for his or her future college and career readiness. [8]

The propaganda regarding tests that have become an unrealistic arbiter of developmental success is far reaching. It would behoove every parent, and indeed, every citizen, to research this concept. The fact is, we have been manipulated over the last 15 years into believing that how students fare on these Common Core tests is the be all and end all to education success. The concern from all quarters regarding the increasingly poor performance on them has caused national angst for years.

Setting aside the advanced nature of the material, there's an additional and very practical reason our students are lagging in their test performance. You might be surprised at how simple it is. I hope you'll stay tuned for *Testing, Part Two* later in this book.

I'll leave you with this thought for now: everything in education policy rides on the performance that students give on the day they test. Yet accountability for students is non-existent. That disconnect is illogical.

A big debate for a long time has been whether to make testing count for students. As you might imagine, I am all for it. That would really change the landscape.

---

[8] https://www.testprep-online.com/parcc-grades-3-4-5

The objective of school-based budgeting (SBB) is to improve school funding by increasing revenues and reducing systemwide costs...

It cannot be assumed that School-Based Budgeting will be effective in every school system, and the proposed cost-benefit model should be applied to the particular facts and circumstances of a school system before adopting it. [9]

---

[9] Chan, Lionel. School-Based Budgeting: A Cost-Benefit Model. 1997. Abstract of a position paper.

6 Murky Waters

The school-based budget entered our lives in the fall of 2014. From the start, it felt like a shady way to manage funding, offering multiple avenues to misrepresent how money was allocated.

Here's what it meant to us:

- The principal is given a certain amount of money per grade level, based on enrollment. This is an incentive to pack classrooms with open-enrolled students.
- The principal can reclaim parts of the money she allocates to classrooms at her discretion.
- The district no longer pays for substitute teachers. That money comes out of each grade level's budget. We were subtly discouraged from using our sick days because it would 'take away from the children'.
- The school budget must pick up a certain portion of the benefits a teacher receives. This, of course, detracts from the school-level items that can be purchased. I saw our budget for allowable teacher requests plummet after the school-based budget was enacted.
- Each grade level budget needed to pay all school fees, including field trips, for those students on Free and Reduced Lunch status, a federal program that extends as an unfunded mandate to states and school districts.

The shortfall of money resulting from students on F & R severely impacted the sixth grade because our major field trip for the year was an outdoor science camp in the mountains. [1] Parent cost was around $300 per student for this week-long curricular requirement. Parents were encouraged to start making small payments for this as early as third grade. Any child on F & R did not have to pay. Prior to the new budget, those funds came from some source at the district level; our school monies were not affected.

After the budget was implemented, our school had to fill in the gaps. In addition to the official F & R students, there were always parents who refused to pay, on principle. Those children still attended, with the cost paid by our sixth-grade budget. [2]

Teachers were also discouraged from making practical and realistic supplies lists to help parents shop for back-to-school, because our budget would have to pay for all the supplies on that list for any student on F & R.

Do you know how easy it is to qualify for F & R? Of course, there are a lot of people who need it. But there are also a lot who take advantage of a federal program designed for abuse. The part in my book *Finishing School* that shares a conversation between Wendy and one of the secretaries about the farce of F & R really happened as I reported it. I'll give you the quick version here:

I had entered the office to turn in an F & R form handed to me by a parent and received an earful from the secretary about how that parent had arrived at school in a Cadillac Escalade to enroll her son, *parking in a red* zone!

I was curious and asked for more information, which the secretary readily shared. This parent was dressed to the nines and smelled of expensive perfume. After parking her Escalade illegally in front of the school, she had sashayed into the office to inform the receptionist at the front desk that she was transferring her son from the neighboring school district and wanted the form for "free stuff".

The secretary told me she had given the lady the correct form but would not be sending it to the district until the deadline was near. She apparently had 30 days to 'process' the form at the school level. When I asked why she would wait, she said, "Did you look at the mother? Would *you* believe she needs 'free stuff'?"

The secretary further informed me that the district just stamps all forms "approved" if the income reported matches the table provided directly on

---

[1] Free or Reduced Lunch Program, a federal program that provides free or reduced-priced meals for students but also ensures their families pay no fees, including those for field trips and supplies. The second part is an unfunded mandate.
[2] One dad told me in 2002 that he would never pay for a field trip, even though he was a journalist and his wife a psychologist. Taxes should pay for everything, he said.

the form. When I asked why the district would do that, I was told it would cost more to staff an office to verify forms than to just okay them. Besides, the federal program pays for the meals, so what does it matter?

I had said, "But we pay for everything else! It does matter."

The secretary had smiled wryly at me. "Not to the district," she told me.

I left the office shaking my head, resolving to write this account up as soon as possible.

The issue of money in education causes a lot of eye rolls and consternation among the public, and it should. There is shady dealing going on; I'm sure what I have witnessed is just the tip of the iceberg.

Several years later, in my final two years before retirement, we had a new principal who latched onto the Rick DuFour mania surrounding PLC's. [3]

To be fair, PLC's do have merit. I saw a seminar given by Rick DuFour (the founder of this movement) around 2002 when he visited our district. I was instantly on board because the whole point of a PLC is to get teachers talking to each other about student need. Mr. DuFour showed videos of what can happen for a struggling high school student when the subject teachers pick up the phone to call each other on behalf of the student. (What he didn't address was the logistics of doing that for 30 or more struggling students among the 150 a high school teacher works with.)

Near the end of his first year with us, this new principal announced that he wanted to take ten teachers to a Rick DuFour conference in Chicago the following summer. Airfare, hotel, meals, and conference cost would be paid for. Upon their return, they would share their experience with the rest of us. I wondered why we couldn't just watch some Rick DuFour videos. There might even have been some from that very conference that we could watch after they were released. Then everyone could get the information, and we could discuss it immediately upon viewing it.

That didn't seem as important as being able to say that 20% of our faculty had personally attended a Very Important Conference, so off they flew to Chicago in June to attend five days of sessions, to the tune of at least $60,000, although the actual tab was never shared with the faculty. Where that money came from is anyone's guess. These teachers reported out to the

---

[3] PLC: Professional Learning Communities. Visit Solution Tree at https://www.solutiontree.com/richard-dufour.html

rest of us in August, making me wonder how useful that timing was. By the time the ladies shared their experiences with us, the information was two months old. (I really hope the principal got his money's worth for this feather in his cap.)

Then there was the disconnect between what was presented to us and what I already knew about PLC's. It seemed that either Rick DuFour had changed the definition, or our principal was cherry-picking concepts that suited his agenda: we were told that for discussions about student need to be meaningful, we would all have to agree on what those students needed to learn. That meant parsing the curriculum prior to anything else.

I spent that school year in weekly meetings with my math colleagues, poring over the district's math curriculum, pulling from it what was necessary for our students to learn and creating our own assessments collaboratively. The two colleagues teaching language arts did the same for the reading curriculum.[4] In effect, we were creating our own curricula that were to be followed every year after that. We would have to spend the next few years doing the same for the writing, social studies, and science curricula. We never once discussed a struggling student that year.

Why were we compelled to parse the curriculum and create our own assessments? Because our principal had insisted that it was the only way to create teacher buy-in, a necessary aspect of effective teaching. My thought was, *What if we change what we teach next year, and I had no say in the reading curriculum. Do we start from square one again?*

What we were doing made no sense. The direction to *"pull from the curriculum what was necessary for our students to learn"* seemed redundant. We were teaching from a district-approved math textbook, which means someone at a higher level than us had already decided what our students needed to learn. And why couldn't we use assessments that had already been created for us?

I mentioned it before in this book: What was the bang for the buck? Why were teachers spending much of their planning time reinventing the wheel? Everything we had been doing for five years felt like mere compliance.

---

[4] By this time, the sixth grade had become partially departmentalized. I taught math and social studies that year.

This pointless exercise underscores the cynicism many teachers feel toward school management. If a principal has chosen a path to future stardom (not difficult to ascertain), a lot of what he requires from his teachers is designed to make himself look good to the muckety-mucks at the top.[5] Hence my earlier comment about the feather in his cap.

---

[5] More evidence that this principal was using our school as a stepping stone to future stardom can be found on page 177.

No matter what form you choose, the most important aspect to consider is how well that evidence you gather responds to your research question. [6]

---

[6] From *Gathering Evidence: Making Student Learning Visible*. Vanderbilt University Center for Teaching, 2013

7 Data for Data's Sake

In the fall of 2012, our principal introduced a year-long, district-wide data collection requirement that she said was inspired by John Hattie's effect size calculator. Being in the meeting where it was introduced felt like being an extra in a Saturday Night Live skit. [1] We were told we had to track our students' growth in three areas: oral skills, written work, and projects. Every three weeks, we were to have a graded project, a major written assignment, and an oral rating submitted on the spreadsheet provided for us.

I could hear the murmurings around me as my colleagues considered the idea of collecting data like this. A project every three weeks? I wondered what was expected for collecting oral data – observational notes or an actual speech?

As if reading my thoughts, our principal Rebecca had continued, "For the oral component, for instance, you can track how your students respond to group discussions in class."

That didn't seem cumbersome at all. I could see myself holding a clipboard in front of the room while I taught, taking the time to make a mark next to the name of someone who contributed in a profound way. (Did anyone think these things through?) I did try it in class a few times during direct instruction of science. As you might imagine, my students were amused. Some of them even tried to help: *That was a great comment, Ms. Zempel. You should mark it down.*

George had raised his hand in that meeting, saying, "So you want work samples submitted?", and I thought, *Yes, George, of course she does!*

---

[1] *Saturday Night Live,* a satirical sketch comedy show, created by Lorne Michaels for NBC Television, 1975.

"No," Rebecca had responded. "We don't have time to look over what your students are doing. That's for you to do. What we want is a record of your scores."

This was when we discovered that no written work was expected to back up the scores we reported; in fact, our principal was adamant that we *not* burden her with anything other than scores on a grid. I remember the moment of quiet after that announcement, as if everyone was afraid to breathe lest Rebecca realize what she had just said.

Even George, who usually had very little filter in our meetings, was mute.

"We've made a template for you as an on-going data record that you'll add to throughout the year," Rebecca had continued, pointing to an image of it on the screen behind her.

"What about project-based data?" George persisted. "Aren't projects usually accompanied by written or oral work, anyway?"

I wanted to chuckle at that question, but the expression on Rebecca's face dissuaded me.

She replied in clipped tones, "Of course, George. But projects are to be distinguished from written and oral data in that they include critical thinking skills."

George looked like he wanted to say more but was thinking better of it.

"Look, people, "Rebecca admonished with her stern voice. "This is to be a useful tool for monitoring the progress of your students." She paused as if selecting her words carefully. "We are in the business of measuring growth. Our job is to assist in that endeavor. This is a directive from the district and from me."

Gathering her notes, she then announced that she would be leaving but her instructional coach would explain the spreadsheet and requirements more fully.

I thought it was cowardly of Rebecca to throw her instructional coach to the wolves like that. The questions that poor lady fielded while attempting to explain what Rebecca wanted were brutal. (I noticed that teachers were far more bold when Rebecca was out of the room.) I wish I still had that spreadsheet, but it didn't occur to me at the time to make a copy or try to email it to myself. At the end of the year, our access was stripped, and I didn't much care. It had been such an odious thing that I was happy to be rid of it. [2]

---

[2] This data requirement also appears in chapter 11 of my first book, *Finishing School*.

The data gathering it represented didn't mesh with our curricular planning. The fact that we had to have a major project graded every three weeks meant that we had to skip lessons in science and social studies (because you certainly can't in math). Planning these projects was one more thing to meet about, and now that I think about it, that's probably the main reason the learning posters from chapter 3 went by the wayside!

There didn't seem to be any use for this data collection, at least any that might benefit a teacher's instruction or a student's learning. And the way it was explained was so vague, I wondered if Rebecca had been given the assignment from *her* bosses only minutes before presenting it to us.

Here is an example of how the grid on the spreadsheet looked, from my best recollection:

Oral Assessment

Student	9/14	10/5	10/26	11/16	12/14
M.C.	2		2	2	2
N.C.	2	2	3	3	3
T.G.	2	2	2	3	3

There is no labeling of assessments to match the dates or data. Just a collection of supposed proficiency marks. [3] They could have represented the number of times I visited the ladies' room that day, for all anyone knew.

It is also not clear whether these scores were based on cumulative observation for a three-week period, or a one-time assessment, such as an oral report delivered in front of the class. Similar grids were filled out for written work and projects, again with no labeling as to what the scores represented.

Above the table was a formula for calculating the effect size, but we were told we didn't have to worry about using it. I was glad, because the instructions that were written above it weren't any clearer than what the

---

[3] Proficiency marks are not grades. They indicate how close a student is to grade level. A '3' is grade level. A '2' is below grade level. A '4' means advanced thinking. A '1' would be two or more grades behind. See chapter 8, p. 79, for more.

instructional coach was saying about it. Distant memories of it returned when I researched online and found this:

$$\text{Effect Size} = \frac{[\text{Mean of experimental group}] - [\text{Mean of control group}]}{\text{Standard Deviation}}$$

It is hard to tell *what* the district's end game was, because we didn't seem to be following any of the protocols for data collection regarding effect size, including the explanation below, from the same paper where I found the effect size calculator above.

Steps for calculating effect size:
1. Arrange student data into columns (Fall and Spring for grade and intervention groups).
2. Insert column and calculate difference between spring and fall for each group (Growth).
3. Use the function capability and calculate the SD and mean of each column.
4. Use the obtained numbers and complete the formula. Effect size is typically reported to two decimal places.
5. Using mean and SD [Standard Deviation] of the national sample, calculate an effect size from intervention to national sample. This adds complexity but allows for a comparison between local and national data. It is possible that the local intervention group will not close the gap with the local grade level yet students are growing more than expected relative to national norms. [4]

This is from a thesis written for school psychologists who might wish to use Hattie's effect-size analyses for determining what works with students and what does not. Included in the thesis is the insistence on valid data for the study, something our district did not appear to understand. Reporting supposed scores on mystery assignments does not seem like 'valid data'.

I cannot imagine how the scores we submitted could possibly be used in any Hattie-style research, anyway, since the growth they supposedly represented had nothing to do with *delivery of instruction*. The entire enterprise seemed pointless, and I was thankful it disappeared after that school year.

---

[4] Birr, Chris and Todd Hrenak. "Using Effect Size to Assess Impact: Be the 'John Hattie' of Your School." 2015

There is still the mystery of *what* it is about Hattie's effect sizes research that is so compelling. In my quest to understand, I found this blog written by Dr. Chris Balow for *Illuminate Education*. (If you read his entire entry from the website in the footnote below, you'll get a succinct summary analysis of Hattie's work.)

> One of the most commonly used scenarios for effect size is to determine the efficacy of an intervention or educational practice relative to a comparison group or approach. Not only does the effect size indicate if an intervention would work, but it also predicts how much impact to expect in a range of scenarios. [5]

What immediately jumps out at me is the phrase *efficacy of an intervention or educational practice relative to a comparison group or approach.* How is that possible to definitively calculate?

Here's a potential research scenario: teachers in one room are teaching using PowerPoint and those in another room are not. Everything else is equivalent in the rooms: placement of furniture, lighting, lesson plans, materials used, instructional techniques, and so on. Perhaps even, the same room is used to deliver the instruction. The purpose is to measure the efficacy of using PowerPoint as a teaching tool. [6]

The learning situations are identical except for the implementation of PowerPoint in one of the rooms. But are they *really* identical? Even if the same group of teachers delivers the instruction, there are still *two groups of children,* and contained within those two groups are unique traits and demeanors. Additionally, how can any researcher control the other factors affecting individual children in an authentic school setting, [7] such as poverty, home life, nuclear family or not, diet, exercise, and motivation, in order to measure *just* the inclusion of PowerPoint on learning outcomes?

I have used PowerPoint as a teaching tool quite successfully (I thought), and I have also used it unsuccessfully. Its efficacy has been very much influenced by the dynamics of the groups I've used it *with,* and even by *my own demeanor* on lesson day.

---

[5] Balow, Chris. "The 'Effect Size' in Educational Research: What is it & How to Use it?" 2017. www.illuminateed.com/blog/2017/06/effect-size-educational-research-use/

[6] According to John Hattie, the use of PowerPoint has an efficacy of +0.26, or 26% of a standard deviation, giving it a fairly small effect on learning

[7] It seems apparent that most educational research is conducted in controlled settings, much like a laboratory. Even in real classrooms, research outcomes would be influenced simply by student awareness that one is under observation.

Regardless, I still consider it a powerful visual aid for concept presentation. It would take more than an effect size assigned by Dr. Hattie to convince me otherwise.

Dr. Balow's final paragraph appears to mirror this stance:

> ...care must be taken with respect to interpreting effect size for educational programs and interventions. The word "effect" connotes or implies "causality" ... In many cases, there is an identified relationship, but the word 'effect' should be used only if it can be justified.
>
> We must also be careful when comparing or aggregating John Hattie [style] effect sizes when there are:
> 1. Different operationalizations of the same outcome.
> 2. Clearly different treatments.
> 3. Measures derived from different student populations.
> 4. Different levels of the same intervention applied. [8]

I think it's safe to say that numbers 2, 3, and 4 will always apply when evaluating any teaching strategy.

What our district put us through couldn't have been a meta-study of different strategies used. It appeared to be a report on growth in proficiency only, regardless of educational practice. Perhaps, even, officials wanted to compare schools against each other within the district. Can anyone see how this might inspire a principal to inflate her scores prior to reporting them?

At the end of the year, our principal included the growth in our scores in the narrative portion of our final evaluation, despite reassuring us in September that that would not be the case.

I noticed a level of distrust take hold between teachers and administration, including the instructional coach, who was neither admin nor teacher. She was regarded more as a mole, and most people were careful what they said around her.

A schism also slowly developed among teachers. Some of them presented a façade of withdrawal: don't say too much in the wrong company. Others, a very small group, took every opportunity to share their positive

---

[8] Balow, 2017.

association with every change thrust upon us and how it was empowering everyone in their classrooms.

The rest fell somewhere in between, trying to affect a participatory presence that was good enough to appease while not drawing unwanted attention.

My skepticism was palpable, I'm sure. I could not sit in meetings and pretend nothing was amiss. The only other teacher who was as outspoken as I was George, the eighth-grade colleague whose comments also appear in chapters 4 and 9, and who inspired a supporting character in *Finishing School*.

Many times during that awful school year, I thought of Dr. Tomlinson's stance on teaching and learning:

- What we study is essential to the structure of the discipline;
- What we study provides a roadmap toward expertise in a discipline;
- What we study is essential to building understanding in the discipline; and
- What we study balances knowledge, understanding, and skill. [9]

I don't know of a single colleague who believed what we were doing was *'essential to the structure of the discipline'* or *'provided a roadmap toward expertise'*, yet we all complied mindlessly. Did any teachers just enter imaginary scores? I am certain of it. If the assignments had no labels, and therefore could not be tracked or verified, why not?

When you are overwhelmed with non-teaching requirements that you perceive have no value *and* you realize there's an end around, you're apt to quietly take the shortcuts that are available. That's human nature.

And because our supervisors never asked to see any of the assessments that those scores represented, it seemed clear the only thing they cared about was the data to report to their *own* supervisors.

Hence, ***data for data's sake***

---

[9] Tomlinson. *Fulfilling the Promise*, p. 60.

I never teach my pupils; I only attempt
to provide the conditions in which
they can learn. [10]

                                            - Albert Einstein

---

8 Nuts and Bolts

The Class Size War

When the education of our nation's young people is at stake, we toss together into one classroom every possible learning strength and disability, and expect a single teacher to be able to work academic miracles with every kid. [1]

Dr. James Delisle

What no one tells you in your teacher training is that the most significant indicator of how your school year will go is something called 'class dynamics'.

In years where everything meshes, you wonder why you ever thought teaching was difficult. I have had perhaps five of those out of 33 years teaching. Every day is sunshine; every moment is a chance to revel in how lucky you are to be blessed with such wonderful student specimens. Well, maybe that is overstating it a bit.

But not by much.

It is not that students are making your life easier; teaching is still a lot of work, and sometimes you still get frustrated that the perfect lesson you planned fizzled during implementation.

No. It's that the students don't have to deal with the distraction of miscreants whose sole purpose appears to be making everyone else unhappy. Students figure out a way to work with each other, even when they don't want to. There's still the odd off day, but it's not the norm. The students get along, for the most part. They do what they should, for the most part. They seem to enjoy their life. And their parents back you up, for the most part. If a student is lazy, he is quietly so and only hurts himself.

---

[1] Delisle, James. "Differentiation Doesn't Work." 2015.

In other years, you try daily to use all behavior modification techniques you have learned to reign in the troublemakers. All it takes is one kid to derail the serenity of working productively. And usually, it's more than one child. That first one acts as a catalyst, emboldening others to jump on his bandwagon.

Then there are the students who cannot really help their behavior, such as those on the autism spectrum. You feel for them because they are in a situation not of their choosing and entirely out of their comfort zone. My student Aaron Ingram [2] was one of those. The mere fact that they are in a classroom of 30 children causes them angst. And they are being taught by someone who doesn't really understand them. The other children tend to give them a wide berth, extending the discomfort. Some of the compassionate kids try to help, but is that really their job?

A handful of kids end up taking most of the teacher's time because of their special needs or demands. Those kids who are not taxing end up as buffers for those who are.

Is this fair? Not at all. But it's a reality, given the way we pack kids into classrooms regardless of how it might affect them.

The old timers who have become principals or other upper management insist it's ludicrous that a classroom can possibly be overcrowded. If there's room for the furniture, then the class size is manageable. This type of thinking is endemic among people who have the luxury of imposing strictures on others that they themselves need not suffer. If any superintendent today had to employ effective differentiation for 30 students *by himself* for an entire school year and then be judged for his efforts, this attitude would undergo serious re-thinking.

One thing that teachers know about class dynamics
(and every administrator denies) is that the number of children
in a confined space seriously affects their ability to work together.

The floor plan on the opposite page represents an elementary school classroom. This arrangement accounts for the different needs of learners, whether they be assigned to work in pairs, groups, or alone. The students in this classroom move around according to what the teacher has planned, so while their belongings might stay at their home desk, *they* often do not.

---

[2] Not his real name; his story, however, appears in my book *Finishing School.*

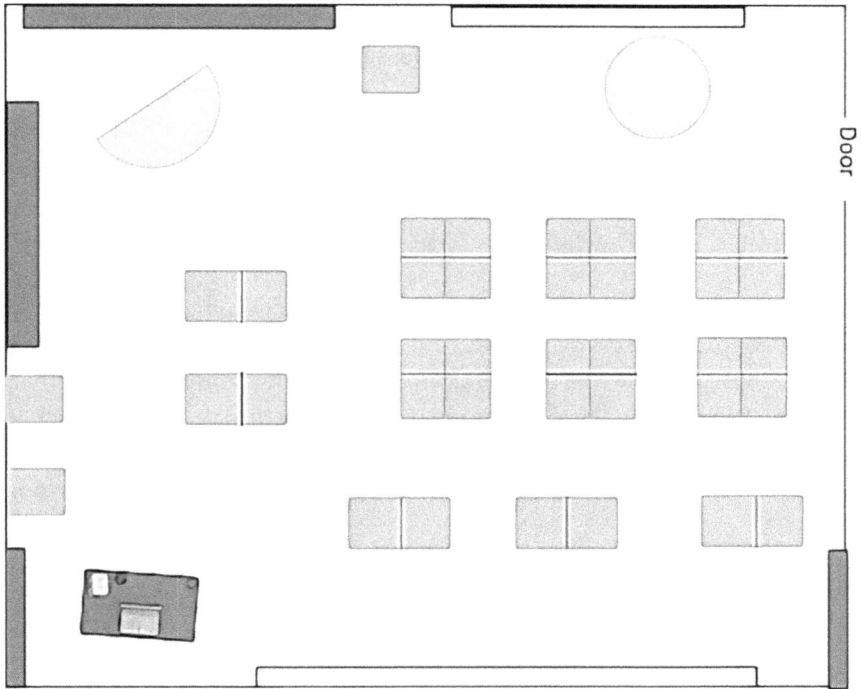

Try putting 30 adults in this 30' x 30' room and asking them to remain productively focused on their own task, ignoring what's going on around them. Assign some of them to discuss ideas in small groups of four. Give others a solo task to complete either on paper or their laptop. Ask others to study or proofread a project silently, while still others take turns reading their projects aloud with a partner. At the same time, try to chair a committee of four while monitoring the activities of everyone else in the room.

Now imagine that some of these people cannot complete their task without supervision or guidance. Others do not want to complete their task because it's more fun to play Minecraft on the tablet they sneaked in. Or throw paper airplanes and trip people who walk by. Or whisper about that kid over there. Others are just tired, so they withdraw at their own desk, hoping no one will notice.

The difference between adults and children in this scenario is that the adults are motivated to keep their job. They are more likely to do what is asked of them. What motivation do children have? Nothing is riding on what *they* do, and they know it. Pushing themselves beyond what is comfortable is not likely.

The experts will assure you that if you would only *train* your students at the beginning of the year, it will be possible for multiple activities to run simultaneously without any disturbances. And it is true that there are teachers who are very good at this. **Being good at maintaining order, though, does not guarantee effective independent learning**. Are those students who are displaying good behavior also challenging themselves to learn to their utmost potential? Is student engagement in an independent task a *given*?

When we examine what happens in a classroom, we must look beyond the level of cooperation on display and ascertain what is driving each student. Being compliant does not necessarily mean being enthusiastic or hard-working. When we make the learning important to the students, we increase the chance that independent activities *will* lead to effective results. At present, teachers are the only people held accountable for student learning.

Let's return to the scenario of 30 adults working in a space like this, trying to be productive, but many of them needing the supervisor's attention. As well as helping each worker, the supervisor also must report what he has done to help. When do you think he's going to do that? Later, after the work shift is over? How will he remember everything he did?

It makes more sense to always have a laptop open and the documentation program available. Then the supervisor can report it the minute he finishes a task.

Now suppose the supervisor realizes he cannot address the needs of every worker, but this might not matter since *his* supervisor cannot possibly match the documented notes to specific activities. Consider, for a moment, the ramifications of this in a classroom setting.

If the elites would be honest, they would acknowledge that class size *does* matter, for everyone in the room. During one particularly prosperous time in our district (2001 to 2003) the superintendent made the decision to funnel more money into grades 3 and 4 for a three-year period. She promised to limit class sizes to 20 students so that teachers could devote more time to each pupil, thereby ensuring a better result in reading scores for the district. Did you get that?

The rationale for putting more money into reducing class size was because the superintendent believed it would be best for students!

In my own school, our principal (the one for whom this book is dedicated) went one better: she funneled more aide time to those teachers, as well. My daughter, who was in third grade, benefited tremendously from this, so I couldn't feel too resentful that I was not among the lucky teachers to work under such ideal conditions.

Unfortunately, the district overestimated its slush of funds and rescinded its promise after the second year. I'm sure those teachers felt a bit of culture shock in the third year after having taught in the promised land only the year before.

The point is, class size _does_ matter,
and the power structure knows it.

The more students you teach and the broader their cognitive range, the more planning, grading, analyzing, and documenting you must accomplish. Students begin to look like cattle going through a chute, getting vaccinated, tagged, and logged. You don't see them any longer as individuals; they are part of a group that must be processed.

It may not be right, but it's what happens when the requirements of your job are not doable, _and_ you are rewarded for pretending they are.

It's a concept that is not difficult to grasp, but administrators are fond of trying their best not to.

The Proficiency System

In 2012, our district did away with letter grades at the elementary level (kindergarten through sixth grade), instituting instead a proficiency system to match the scoring system used by our state standardized battery of tests:

> 4 = Advanced (above grade level understanding of concepts)
> 3 = Proficient (at grade level)
> 2 = Partially Proficient (below grade level)
> 1 = Unsatisfactory (two or more years below grade level)

We were told that a 4 did not mean an 'A'. It meant that a child had displayed advanced thinking for his grade level on that indicator. As you might imagine, 4's are rare.

In addition to no longer giving letter grades, we also did not give a rating for a subject as a whole, such as *Reading*. Instead, *Reading* was divided into separate sections called *Indicators of Performance*.

In sixth grade, our indicators for reading included the following in 2012:

- Applies Comprehension Strategies to Understand a Variety of Texts;
- Develops, Transfers, and Applies Word Knowledge Strategies;
- Reads Independently; and
- Oral Reading Fluency.

Our grading systems now had to include separate documents to track each of these indicators. Many assignments would have more than one of the indicators associated with them, so that required putting marks on multiple grids, as well as marking papers with multiple ratings, each of which needed a label. Try to imagine the time it takes to grade an assignment this way. A child could get a 4 for depth of thought in explaining a comprehension strategy, but a 2 for word knowledge and sentence structure. This involves giving both a reading and a writing grade for one assignment. Keeping up with the grids necessary to prove one's ratings on the final report card could become quite time-consuming. I'm sure many teachers just gave out 3's because it was easier that way.

Here's the nonsensical part about proficiency grading:

In a proficiency system, what you want is for students to be proficient for their grade level, marked by a 3. But think about that. There are bound to be high 3's and low 3's, because the gamut of proficiency in any grade level is pretty wide. Just how informative *is* the proficiency system to a child or his parent? In my opinion, it encourages students to aim for 'average', because they know they are unlikely to demonstrate advanced thinking or writing. Putting in extra effort on anything that does not improve their rating seems a waste of time.

Around 8% of our population is gifted, and that's really what a 4 means. Yes, it's possible for any person to have a gifted *moment*, but for most kids, they knew that was out of the realm for *them*. They became perfectly content to get their 3's, even if that 3 gave little indication of level of learning.

The fallout from grading students using proficiency marks is that most of them lose the desire to be excellent, something that is possible when you award grades based on effort and merit. This is what many of my colleagues feared would happen, judging by the comments I heard when the system was rolled out.

For those students who cared about grades, many wanted to know why they hadn't earned a *4* when they hadn't made any mistakes on the assignment. Students and parents had a tough time with the concept of *4*, not understanding that it did not equal an *A*. Receiving 100% of the points available on an assignment merely meant that the student completed what was required of him, fully. It did not mean that he showed exceptional depth of thought.

And there were some assignments that it was not possible to get a *4* on, such as completing a math assignment on multiplication. You're expected to know how to multiply everything in sixth grade, so doing it well means you get a *3*. If you show advanced thinking on a word problem, you *might* get a *4*. But even that is very subjective, because the teacher is analyzing your thought process. One teacher on my team insisted that solving word problems is expected, so it was *never* possible to get a *4*. It became one more thing to argue about.

The proficiency system encourages sloppy grading, as well. The savvy teacher soon learned that most of the daily assignments she would ever look at would turn out to be a *3*, so she would begin the grading by sorting the papers in a typecasting way. Certain students could be counted on to understand the concept and complete the assignment as they should. Those went into the *3* pile. Other students were known academic issues. Those went into the *2* pile. It was then a matter of deciding if a *2* was bad enough to actually be a *1* and if anything about the *3* might make it a *4*. That was an even smaller category.

You only had to make detailed markings on a paper that deserved a *1* or *2*. If you eyeballed it and could see that the kid knew what he was doing, you just put a *3* at the top in your green marker.

If you really wanted to help your student understand how he was doing, you could add a plus or a minus to the proficiency range. Some of my students did ask me why their rating was a *3-*, and I took the time to explain why I thought it was just barely at grade level but not poor enough to place them behind in their learning. I always added that they should take it as a warning that a little more effort is probably needed, because that *3-* could turn into a *2* very easily.

Even more difficult for students and parents is that proficiency marks are not averaged. In a proficiency system of grading, what matters is *the growth a child experiences at the end of the grading period*. The teacher keeps the proficiency marks on a grid, and as she analyzes the grid for that student at the end of the quarter, she notices if the marks turn consistently to '3's'. If so, the mark for that indicator will be a 3 on the report card. If not, if there are still more than a few 2's sprinkled in at the end, then the overall rating on the report card is going to be a 2 because growth in learning was not maintained.

"But he has mostly 3's on his assignments!" parents would exclaim. "How can he not have a 3 in this 'Vocabulary' part of his report card?"

"Because his 3's in vocabulary dropped off four weeks ago. He's been doing partially proficient work ever since, and I cannot mislead you into thinking he is performing at grade level," I would say, and then watch them shake their head in disbelief at such nonsense.

Parents sometimes tried to go over our heads to the principal to get marks changed on their child's report card. Rather than accept that the report card is a *report* of their child's acquisition of necessary skills, many parents still thought of it as a reward for hard work. Remember getting paid by your dad for how many *A*'s you got on your report card?

There were few things our principal backed us up on, but our judgment of proficiency marks was among that select group. If the child was not at grade level, she believed the teacher had a responsibility to share that with the parents.

It is not entirely the fault of students and their parents that they couldn't wrap their heads around the proficiency system. We still held awards assemblies, honoring those students who received only 3's and 4's on their report cards, and double honoring those who managed to 'earn' a certain number of 4's. We were providing contradictory information: *Don't think of these marks as merit based, but we're still going to reward your child for his success.*

The point of the proficiency system is to let parents know how their child's development stacks up compared to the grade he is in. Receiving a high number of 2's means the child is behind. The guiding premise in this system is that a teacher can help the learning along, but if it's not the brain's time to master something, the child must be given time and more instruction until he *can* master it, or until his brain *lets* him master it. Rewarding children for their proficiency seems counter to the philosophy behind it.

When it was introduced to us, I did see the usefulness of the proficiency system at the primary level, because it shared with parents whether their children were acquiring the foundational skills they needed. But simply pointing the deficits out to parents is not enough. Those learning gaps must be closed. Leaving the child with the herd is not going to get that done. The gaps will continue to widen. This is because reading instruction takes on different nuances at different grade levels. At one time, I heard a reading specialist put it this way:

> In grades K-3, a child should be *learning to read.* Once he
> reaches fourth grade, however, that changes:
> a child should now be *reading to learn.*

If a child has not progressed by fourth grade to the point that he has the foundational skills necessary to join the *'reading to learn'* crowd, his class placement must reflect this. Expecting a general ed teacher to differentiate for his exceptional needs while teaching true fourth graders the material that is appropriate for *them* is illogical.

For those children in grades 4-6 who have the foundational skills down, development becomes more effort driven. With continued effective instruction, these children should move closer and closer to self-learning. A parallel point is that by fourth or fifth grade, proficiency marks gravitate toward counter-productivity. By that time in a child's life, he needs to receive merit-based grades so that he will learn to value the effort it takes to achieve, and his parents deserve to know whether he is earning high 3's (*A*'s) or low 3's (*C*'s). I could understand everyone's frustration with the system.

Parent-teacher conferences became hugely challenging. I am sure many parents developed a coating of cynical armor gazing at the sea of 3's on their child's report card, wondering whether each represented an *A, B,* or *C.* If parents asked me, I told them what letter grade I would convert a 3 to, but I never brought it up on my own. Why open another can of worms?

An Ethical Dilemma

Every school district requires its teachers to sign some type of conduct agreement. It outlines what we are allowed to do while in the building, how we are allowed to use the equipment, such as the Internet, how and if to accept gifts, what is prohibited on school grounds, such as political discussion, clothing, and the like, and generally, what the non-teaching terms of our contract involve.

In my district, this document is called an Ethics Agreement, and it was required to be digitally signed by October 15 of each school year. Most teachers probably don't read the entire document; it's not exactly riveting. I read it for the first time in 2013 and was stunned to learn that in addition to indicating my understanding of all the policies about not accepting gifts as payment for grades and not using worktime to shop on Amazon, I was also signing an NDA (non-disclosure agreement).

I was prohibited from discussing with anyone outside my school district the policies enacted inside it. This included parents, and the restriction applied to *any* policy at all, regardless of its content.

When our principal brought up the subject of the Ethics Agreement in an early faculty meeting that year, she commented that it is just good policy not to use parents as a sounding board for our own discontent. That leads to low morale for everyone. I could see the logic in that. It's never a good idea to unload when you're upset about something; what you say cannot be taken back.

But it didn't seem from the wording that the NDA's purpose was to keep us from grousing to parents. In fact, the wording was so general, it could have been interpreted in any unexpected way by our bosses. You can see it written in bold and highlighted in gray on the opposite page. When I questioned our principal about that word *'proprietary'*, she reluctantly acknowledged that any information we were provided by the district for the purpose of doing our job would fall under that category, and therefore, could not be shared outside our school walls. **The week after the staff meeting in which Rebecca discussed this agreement, she unveiled the district's new evaluation plan (see chapter 9), all of which was considered *'proprietary'*.**

Why was our school district loath to let the public know what it was doing? Did it consider itself a private corporation without shareholders to answer to? Even worse, was it fearful that if the public was privy to the new evaluation system, they'd have questions about its validity? I thought about the tax dollars that support this 'corporation' and wondered what taxpayers might say about teachers being required to sign an NDA so the 'corporate' bigwigs could act in secret.

This type of requirement is an inappropriate policy, but school districts know they have their teachers over a barrel. Refusing to sign means one will be dismissed from one's job. I wonder how many other school districts require similar NDA's. Maybe you'd like to add that to your list of questions at the next school board meeting.

The Non-Disclosure Part of
An Ethics Agreement
Circa 2013

All employees should be alert for any indication of fraud, financial impropriety or irregularity within his/her areas of responsibility.

Fraud includes but is not limited to:

- Forgery, unauthorized alteration of any document or account;

- Misappropriation of funds, securities, supplies or other assets, including theft, embezzlement, purchasing property for personal use and providing false information to obtain material benefit.

- Unauthorized use of district equipment, facilities, supplies or funds for purposes unrelated to district business.

- Falsification or manipulation of employee expense records or employee time records.

- Impropriety in handling money or reporting financial transactions. Profiteering because of insider information of district information or activities.

- **Disclosure of confidential and/or proprietary information to outside parties.**

- Acceptance or seeking of anything of material value, other than items used in the normal course of advertising, from contractors, vendors or persons providing services to the district.

- Destruction, removal or inappropriate use of district records, furniture, fixtures, or equipment.

- Failure to provide financial reports to authorized state or local entities. Failure to cooperate fully with financial auditors, investigators or law enforcement.

- Other dishonest or fraudulent acts involving district monies or resources.

See also Appendix B, page 218.

Bureaucracy:
the administrative system governing any large institution,
whether publicly owned or privately owned. [3]

Some people take themselves very seriously. This appears
especially applicable to those who cherish
their place in the bureaucracy.

---

[3] Wikipedia: Bureaucracy definition: https://en.wikipedia.org/wiki/Bureaucracy

9 Performance Evaluation

Document Everything

In the spring of 2012, as she was looking at her retirement from education, outgoing Assistant Principal Rose Keebler, gave me a private heads-up.

We had been sitting in her office, going over my final evaluation. I had thanked her for her support over the years and wished her well in her next venture.

Then I made a remark that changed everything. "It's not as if it really matters, career-wise," I said to her, "but I do appreciate all the good things you've said about how I teach."

She had smiled grimly. "Everything's changing," she had said. "Soon, it *will* matter."

"What do you mean?" I asked. "Isn't the evaluation process just a formality? Practically like having a tea party with your supervisor at the end of the year?"

"For you, yes," Rose had agreed. "That's how it's been. But believe me, there's a lot of talk about the teachers who aren't good. Everyone at the top is sick and tired of the complacency. If you're not documenting everything, you should start now."

I had raised my eyebrows at that. "Come on, Rose," I protested. "How feasible is that? I'd never have time to teach."

"You have no idea what you'll need to find time to do. Next year, everything changes."

Even as I tried to get her to tell me more, she demurred. I was left to wonder what was coming down the pike. I had the summer to stew about it.

The next school year, Gary Morris, who had been hired two years earlier to be AP for grades K-4, took Rose's place as AP for grades 5-8. School year 2012-13 was also the last time Rebecca assigned herself as my evaluator, giving that task to Morris beginning in 2013. It was in early September when he introduced us to the online documentation system.

"You'll need to document for every student on an IEP or ALP,[1] but it would behoove you to include everyone you work with," he said. "And you can do bulk documentation, as well. Just choose your group of students and write something down for all of them. Our world is now about documentation. If it isn't written down, it didn't happen."

I began spending my lunch period eating at my desk, writing things online and in my digital files. Here is a typical entry:

9/20/2012	Ethan M.	Small group instruction
	Mandy K.	on main idea and details.
	Ralph G.	
	Tony B.	20 minutes

The steps for creating this documentation were incredibly simple. Once logged into my teacher account, I chose the option for NEW and typed my instruction into a text box. Then I checked off the students I wanted to apply it to. There were a few other parameters to fill out, such as the date of the supposed instruction and the length of time it took. The finished product looked like what you see above. Morris had told us he could monitor our activities from his own account.

I wondered if anyone would know if I fabricated what I typed into the system. But how *could* they?

One day several years later (fall of 2017), while my aide was in my room, I asked her to monitor independent work so I could run down the hall and ask a colleague something. When I entered the room, I saw students working quietly at their desks, writing in spiral notebooks. My colleague was at her desk, on her computer, typing. She glanced up at me warily. I approached her desk, and she turned her monitor slightly. The movement didn't affect me one way or the other until much later, when I thought seriously about how teachers could possibly do all the individual instruction that their documentation attested to.

At this point, we had all been working under the strictures of our new normal for five years. Almost no one could remember a time when we weren't making educator goals for our kids, gathering growth data, or documenting.

[1] ALP: Advanced Learning Plan: for students testing into the Gifted and Talented Program

I often heard hushed comments like *"How do they think we're going to get all this done? And what about discipline? Does anyone care that at least five of my students routinely ruin learning for everyone else?"*

In an early meeting, I pointed out that not all our students care about learning targets or success criteria and was cut off by an irate principal, who said crisply, "They care about *something*. And they *are* curious. It's *your* job to find out what motivates them."

It was not pleasant to be on the receiving end of that; others noticed, and it effectively shut down much publicly voiced dissent thereafter. (You'll remember I mentioned a similar occurrence on page 31, related to the disconnect between Dr. Tomlinson's and Dr. Hattie's theories.)

In other meetings, I was lost in thought observing my colleagues: those who were weary and close to retirement; those who were new to the profession and looked perpetually stressed; and those who were full of ambition – becoming yes-men to everything in an effort to ingratiate themselves. I wondered what this third faction *really* did in their classrooms, when their boss was no longer present to be impressed by their enthusiasm.

District experts were brought in to give us encouraging presentations on the data that supports everything we were doing, feeding us phrases steeped in empathy:

"We feel your frustration."

"We know that you need more than you're getting. We want to help."

Empty words.

Beginning in 2012, we became inundated with buzzwords like *'work smarter, not harder'*, *'research-based'*, *'data driven'*, and *'what's best for kids'*. Rebecca often talked about us *'improving our practice'*.

My thoughts have evolved toward the theory that communication like this was necessary to get us on board with a planned massive overhaul, implemented strategically.

Stage one: Convince us that our job was more complex than we had previously thought; ongoing training and retraining were necessary.

Stage two: Guide us into believing that data collection and documentation were more important than how we interacted with our students.

Stage three was the most insidious: Make us doubt our own common sense.

I never saw defeat and weariness in people like I did between the years 2012 and 2014.

Effectiveness Matrix

In September 2012, the faculty assembled for our usual Wednesday meeting. The agenda had listed Evaluation as the last item. The noise from teachers enjoying their usual inane conversations prior to a meeting seemed to me wholly out of place. I kept staring at that word Evaluation and hoping Rose had been wrong.

The room quieted down as our principal Rebecca arrived. She walked to the podium and set her stack of notes on it. Then she looked around at the assembled teachers and smiled.

"**Hello, everyone,**" she began. "How good it is to be back for a new year, working with our excited students." She punctuated that remark with a bright smile.

"We as educators have a unique responsibility to assist them in their endeavor to become educated. Our learning goals and learning targets must be reflective of the end goals that these little human beings strive for in their lives. Helping them achieve their goals is a time-honored endeavor that those outside the profession can never truly comprehend."

"But as we work toward those daily learning targets, we must remember that true learning doesn't exist without a vision of success criteria for our students."

I doodled around the words on my agenda, drawing circles and stars.

"Those criteria might take many forms," Rebecca continued, looking around the room. "It could be a paragraph written in their journal that explains from their own point of view what they learned from the lesson. It could be an oral discussion of their learning or an exit slip on which they summarize the key points of the lesson."

Blah, blah, blah, I thought.

"And as we prepare for our new year of instructing our students, we, the administrators and instructional personnel of this school, will help you unpack your own learning in an effort to assist you in your own endeavors to become the most effective educators that you can be."

"Today, we'll focus on new policies from the district, based on Senate Bill 10-191, also known as the Educator Effectiveness Act." Rebecca paused, clearing her throat.

Finally, she appeared to be edging toward evaluation.

"With the advent of this new school year, we begin the challenge to raise the bar on our Evaluative Procedures." Rebecca pointed to the graphic on the screen behind her and stepped aside so we could see it.

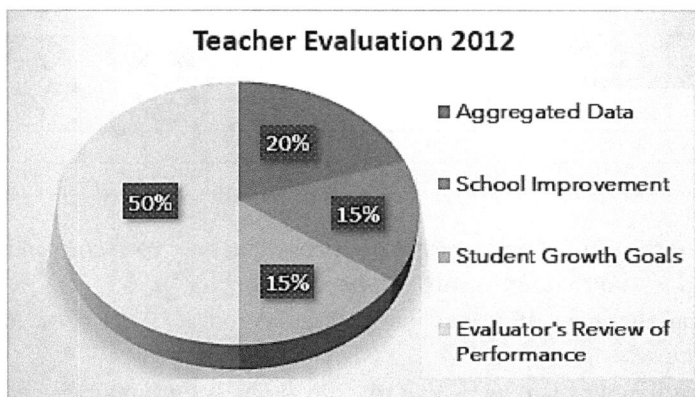

I stared at the pie chart on the screen, wondering what '20% Aggregated Data' meant. My colleague Mary is the one who noticed the Growth Goals.

"*Aggregated Data* includes your standardized test scores from last year. Plus a composite of the standardized scores for every teacher in the building," Rebecca clarified for us.

Eyebrows raised around the room.

"What questions come to mind as you look at this graph?" Rebecca asked.

George stood up. "I'm having a tough time with it," he said. "Am I the only one who notices that we're being held accountable for what our colleagues do?"

Rebecca smiled. "None of us operate in a vacuum, George," she said. "The progress of any student can be attributed to the efforts of every teacher who has worked with him, from the time he was in kindergarten."

"What about those students who haven't been with us since kindergarten?" George persisted.

"Senate Bill 10-191 was written to help you improve your practice," Rebecca said, ignoring his question. "Every teacher should want that as a top priority in his profession."

George spoke as if something new had occurred to him. "How does this new system affect tenure?" he asked.

"The district has decided that tenure no longer exists," Rebecca said. "In order to inspire the younger teachers and to be fair to everyone involved, every teacher will be evaluated every year against this chart." She clicked her remote and another slide appeared on the screen. It was color-coded to show various levels of something called 'Educator Effectiveness Matrix'.

Educator Effectiveness Matrix Compare this table with the raw score on your final evaluation to determine your overall rating.			
Highly Effective			
Effective			
Partially Effective			
Ineffective			
0-12.5	12.6-25	25.1-37	37.1-50

"Your rating of effectiveness will be based on how you score on this chart," she said. "And that final score will be all up to you."

"What happens if a teacher is rated Partially Effective or Ineffective?" someone asked.

"If it happens two years in a row, he or she is put on a two-year program for improvement," Rebecca said. "In that time, he must show growth."

"Growth according to who?" someone else muttered.

Rebecca smiled grimly. "People," she said, "you've been evaluated by an administrator *how* many years in your career?" She paused as if choosing her words carefully. "You will still have observations throughout the year—and you will still make goals."

"The same goals we've had before?" Maureen from third grade asked.

Rebecca nodded. "Similar. We'll talk about that next week. In the meantime, please keep in mind that this system has been created and implemented for your benefit. It gives you control over your own evaluations and salary increases."

"How does it do that?" George asked, sounding skeptical.

"The district wants to reward your efforts and achievements," Rebecca said. "So...you'll be getting percentage increases in salary for next school year based on where you place on this Effectiveness Matrix at the end of this school year. Well, not this year. This is just a dry run. A sort of dress-rehearsal for the district."

"My salary will be tied to this matrix that includes my *colleagues'* test scores and my evaluator's *subjective* comments about me?"

Rebecca's patience appeared to wear thin. "It all makes sense, George," she told him. "You'll see."

"What if I do everything right and my hard work still doesn't make a difference in my students' growth?"

That one came from me.

Rebecca had looked at me for a moment. Then she said, "This is why it's a *matrix* of evaluation. It's not only the scores of your students that matter. There's also the student data goals you will make and monitor throughout the year. And don't forget—your evaluator will have a big impact on everything. When you show him how well you teach using best practices, your final evaluation will reflect that." [2]

The New Goal-Setting Protocols

The process of collecting classroom growth data began for us in 2012, a year before our district implemented its new plan, when our principal volunteered our school as a case study for a dry run.

We were to set two learning goals for our classes, taking a baseline first to establish a starting point for growth. Then we would deliver instruction, allow for practice, and monitor student progress across the school year. We were told to use small assessments of, say, 5 questions each and track the raw scores on those assessments. A grid such as the following could be used:

Student	Baseline	Oct	Mar	Final Score
Mark A.	2/5 or 40%	2/5 or 40%	3/5 or 60%	4/5 or 80%
Ellen B.	4/5 or 80%	4/5 or 80%	4/5 or 80%	5/5 or 100%
Karen C.	1/5 or 20%	1/5 or 20%	2/5 or 60%	4/5 or 80%

The increase from baseline to final score is what mattered, and while we were told this exercise would not apply to our evaluations that year, we were surprised to find it mentioned in the narrative portion written by our evaluator in May.

The protocols we followed for this dress rehearsal were extremely simplistic compared to what was rolled out the following year.

In August 2013, Rebecca handed her teachers a thick packet of requirements for setting the student goals we would track for growth across the school year.

---

[2] This unpromising statement inspired the plot twist in *Finishing School*.

Excerpts from that 21-page packet, which I still have, appear on the next several pages:

"All licensed personnel are required to set individual growth goals pertaining to the performance outcomes that are the focus of her/his position. The focus varies by job category. **State regulations require all licensed personnel to identify at least one individual growth goal measured by something other than TCAP**...

Teachers: State statute and rules specify that teachers, or licensed personnel with direct instructional responsibilities, must set goals that pertain directly to gains in student learning in reference to the Colorado Academic Standards and that districts must use student assessment results to measure attainment of these goals...

All educators must set at least one, and up to five, individual growth goals for the 2013-14 school year. Educator attainment of all of his/her individual growth goals will make up 15% of his/her annual overall performance evaluation rating. The report result section includes options for combining data regarding multiple goals...

Steps for Setting and Specifying the Goal(s):

Step One: Specify the Student Population and Instructional Interval
...for most educators, this would include the full term of the class or course (year, semester, and trimester).

Step Two: Specify the Student Learning Goal(s)
...Goals involve the following:

Identify the "big ideas" for the grade level and content area.

Identify learning goals associated with at least one "big Idea" that would be achieved across several units, and/or which have related objectives in prior or subsequent grade levels using the Collaborative Curriculum Alignment Process (C-CAP). These become candidates to be the Learning Goal.

Determine which standards (from the Colorado Academic Standards) are associated with each candidate Learning Goal.

Prioritize possible Learning Goals based on the learning needs of the student population (identifying two or three top priorities).

Determine the Depth of Knowledge (cognitive complexity) of the priority Learning Goals. Eliminate candidate Learning Goals with a Depth of Knowledge less than 2 for elementary and less than 3 for middle or high school.

Select the Learning Goal(s) and describe each in a format that includes a verb and a noun or noun phrase. The verb should describe the intended cognitive process and the noun or noun phrase generally describes the knowledge students are to acquire or construct.

Step Three: Select and Describe the Body of Evidence and Scoring

Educators...must describe the body of evidence they will collect about student learning gains in relationship to the Learning Goal(s) at the end of the instructional interval. This specifically includes identifying the assessment instruments or tasks they will use to collect student learning data and describing how they know that the assessment instruments they are using accurately measure student learning in relationship to their Learning Goal(s).

Step Four: Analyze Baseline Data

Educators should identify at least three data sources they will use to establish the starting point for measuring student learning progress towards the Learning Goal...

Step Five: Set Performance Targets

...Educators write an expected target for each performance group by the end of the instructional period based on the identified body of evidence. Educators must start by specifying the level of performance that constitutes meeting the Learning Goal(s). Educators may determine other levels of performance such as partially meeting or not meeting the target. The educator targets should specify what number or percent of students in each performance group will score at each level on the final evidence source(s). Establishing expected targets for these different student groups for one Learning Goal is part of setting a single growth goal.

Specify How Growth Scores Will Be Calculated

Educators must specify what growth scores will be provided for each student using the identified assessment instrument(s).... Educators and leaders must determine what method(s) will be used to calculate growth scores and if a consistent method will be used across the school.

Step Six: Provide Evidence Regarding the Technical Quality of Growth Scores

Assessment instruments can only measure a subset of what students actually know, understand, and do, related to the Learning Goal(s). As a result, any score produced by an assessment instrument includes some error in measuring student learning in relationship to the Learning

Goal(s)...Appropriate evidence regarding the score reliability depends on the scoring method.

Step Seven: Determine Cut Scores or Comparison Points and Set Performance Targets

...How much growth is enough for each student to make during the instructional interval? This involves establishing performance levels and aggregating performance across the student population.

...As an example, the state of Colorado has established the following ranges to describe different levels of individual student growth using student growth percentiles generated by the Colorado Growth Model.

Colorado Growth Model for TCAP:

INDIVIDUAL STUDENT GROWTH PERCENTILES	
HIGH	at or above the 66th percentile
MEDIUM	at or between the 35th percentile and the 65th percentile
LOW	up to and including the 34th percentile

Once educators have established performance levels for their students' growth scores, they must consider the growth of the student population as a whole and set performance targets. In other words, determine for the class as a whole what number or percent of students will constitute meeting the growth goal...

DETERMINE POINT CALCULATION

Educators in collaboration with their supervisors must specify how to assign the 15 possible points for individual growth goals based on educator attainment of their performance targets. How points are distributed is a local decision. However, the approach taken should be explained and reasonably justified, and a consistent approach for calculating individual growth goal points should apply across the entire school. This calculation depends on two factors: how many individual growth goals the educator has set, and the approach taken to measure the goals.

If educators set more than one goal, educators must then determine how to weight the goals. In general, the calculation should distribute points as evenly as possible across each goal. (e.g. 5 + 5 + 5 or 7 + 8)

Then, educators and their supervisors must establish the distribution of points within each goal based on the performance targets. Consider the following example of the potential scoring for one of three equally weighted goals (worth 5 points):

Score	SAGO [3] Approach Points	Score	Pre and Post Assessment Approach Rules
0	No performance targets met	0	No students with typical or high growth
1	One performance target met	1	At least 25% of students with typical or high growth
3	More than one but not all performance targets met	3	At least 50% of students with typical or high growth
5	All performance targets met	5	100% of students with typical or high growth

The principal must sign-off on all individual educator goals by October 15th." [4]

Are you dizzy yet?

At the time, I supposed this convoluted mess is what the district did not want its teachers sharing with the public; I could see why. I thought of the NDA I had been compelled to sign and realized I couldn't even discuss this with my aide, who was also a school parent.

After giving us the packet of information, Rebecca never referred to it again, at least not in a full-faculty meeting. She and her two assistant principals had divided our faculty of nearly 50 teachers among them for evaluation and began the process of supervising our goal setting.

Gary Morris was my evaluator; he sent an email to the teachers on his list, directing them to reply with a rough draft of their goal proposals. At no point during consultations with him did he mention the procedures suggested in Step Two on pages 94 and 95. In fact, the process we went through was incredibly superficial compared to the directions in our packet.

Once our goals were approved and the baselines given, we were directed to open the district's online form to enter the rest of the required information. When I looked at that form for my first goal, I was struck by how simple it looked compared to the requirements delineated in the packet.

---

[3] SAGO = Student Academic Growth Objectives, defined by state rules as "a participatory method of setting measurable goals, or objectives, for a specific assignment or class, in a manner aligned with the subject matter taught, and in a manner that allows for the evaluation of the baseline performance of students and the measurable gain in student performance during the course of instruction" (1CCR 301-87-1.23)
[4] From a Denver area school district, issued August 2013.

Since I taught all subjects, I decided to split my 15 points for educator goals between language arts and math (8 + 7, respectively).

My language arts goal was to have my students write a proficient essay on this prompt: *Explain the Value of Education in Our Society.* Progress monitoring would include scoring students on other writing prompts throughout the school year. In April, I planned to have students write to the original prompt again, without the benefit of looking at their first writing sample.

I administered the baseline in mid-September, and once it was scored, I began entering information into the online form. Then I submitted it and it was sent electronically to Morris. He reviewed it online and then sent it back to me with suggestions for revisions. We went through this process several times before he finalized my two goals in mid-October.

The table below represents this writing goal. **The criteria in the LEFT COLUMN** are what the district provided on the template. Everything in the **right column was entered by me** and approved by Gary Morris.

Language Arts Goal

GOAL DETAILS	DESCRIPTION
STUDENT GROWTH GOAL STATEMENT	*Students will write an informational essay to explain with a clear focus and well-developed ideas.*
RATIONALE FOR GOAL SELECTION	*Based on our school UIP [5] goal, I have opted to select a writing goal as a primary focus.*
STUDENT POPULATION	*30 students in my writing class*
ASSESSMENT INSTRUMENT(S)	*Pre-and post-assessment essays*
EVIDENCE RE: THE TECHNICAL QUALITY OF THE ASSESSMENT INSTRUMENT(S)	*Students will respond to a writing prompt ("Explain the Value of Education in our Society"). The students' writing responses will be scored using a 4 point rubric, which will be used to evaluate both assessments administered at the beginning and end of the year. My performance target is to increase the percentage of students improving at least one level on the rubric or maintaining a score of 4.*
CALCULATION OF GROWTH SCORES	*Students are expected to increase one level on the rubric or maintain their 4.*
EVIDENCE RE: THE QUALITY OF GROWTH SCORES	*Essays and scores will be reviewed by my evaluator.*

---

[5] Universal Improvement Plan: set and monitored by the principal.

BASELINE FOR MEASURING GROWTH (CUT SCORES)	*3 students are unsatisfactory (= score of 1)* *14 students are partially proficient (= score of 2)* *13 students are proficient (= score of 3)* *0 students are advanced (= score of 4)*
POINTS EARNED CALCULATION:	*8 points: 90% of students increase one level* *7 points: 80-89% of students increase one level* *6 points: 70-79% of students increase one level* *5 points: 60-69% of students increase one level* *4 points: 50-59% of students increase one level* *3 points: 40-49% of students increase one level* *2 points: 30-39% of students increase one level* *1 point: 20-29% of students increase one level* *0 points: fewer than 19% of students increase one level*

The criteria for success was taken from the same proficiency marks we had begun using for our report cards:

    4 = advanced
    3 = proficient (grade level knowledge)
    2 = partially proficient
    1 = unsatisfactory (significantly below grade level)

As you can see in the chart above, more than half my students scored below proficient on their baseline. You may also have noticed the box at the bottom of the previous page, where I wrote that *"Essays and scores will be reviewed by my evaluator"*. That did not happen. Gary Morris did not request either the essays or the scoring grid I had used. (I didn't offer it because I wanted to see if he would**.) I merely reported my percentage rate of success for the final essay *in the online system* in April and he signed off on it.**

I earned four out of the eight points I had allotted for this goal. Out of 30 original students, 26 finished the year with me. Of those 26, 14 improved by one level on the rubric. That is a success rate of 54%. Had I known that no evidence would be required to prove these figures, I might have been tempted to edge that success rate closer to 80% on paper. But perhaps not. Being out of favor can make one quite wary. Think about the possibility of this happening, though, with the thousands of teachers across the district who were preparing their own goal report-outs. [6]

Even without entering fraudulent data into the online system at the end of the year, I could easily have manipulated the way students wrote to their

---

[6] By the time I reported out on my 2013-14 goals, I had already been targeted by Gary Morris, as you'll read in the next chapter.

final prompt by brainstorming ideas with them and helping them to create their outline prior to writing the final essay. I could even have had them turn in a rough draft so I could add ideas to it or suggest better sentence structures before they wrote their final copy. None of the steps for administering this final essay were monitored by anyone. I could have done anything I wanted without repercussion.

The next chart shows the criteria I entered for my math goal, which was to have students write justifications for their math thinking. Gary Morris suggested this goal, saying it would align with the school's Universal Improvement Plan.

Math Goal

GOAL DETAILS	DESCRIPTION
STUDENT GROWTH GOAL STATEMENT	*Student will set up the appropriate equations for a variety of problems in a single assessment.*
RATIONALE FOR GOAL SELECTION	*Students must be able to use logical reasoning to be able to solve mathematical problems. Determining which algebraic equation to use sets the student up for either success or failure in problem solving.*
STUDENT POPULATION	*29 students in my grade-level math class.*
MEASUREMENT APPROACH (ASSESSMENT INSTRUMENTS AND DATA SOURCE)	*An assessment given in April with a variety of "story problems". Students must decide how to set up each problem and offer a written justification for each.*
BASELINE FOR MEASURING GROWTH:	*12 students are unsatisfactory (= score of 1)* *10 students are partially proficient (= score of 2)* *7 students are proficient (= score of 3)* *0 students are advanced (= score of 4)*
POINTS EARNED CALCULATION:	*(7 pts) 28 or better will achieve 90% on the test* *(6 pts) 25 to 27 will achieve 90% on the test* *(5 pts) 22 to 24 will achieve 90% on the test* *(4 pts) 19 to 21 will achieve 90% r on the test* *(3 pts) 16 to 18 will achieve 90% on the test* *(2 points) 13 to 15 will achieve 90% on the test* *(1 pt) 10 to 12 will achieve 90% on the test* *(0 pts): fewer than 10 will achieve 90%*

The student population does not match that from my language arts goal because we ability-grouped for math. My 29 math students were considered 'grade level'. Other teachers taught the advanced and remedial classes.

I earned five out of the seven points available: 23 of my students achieved at least 90% on the final test. Notice that students were not graded on *solving* the equations, only setting them up correctly and explaining their thinking. (And again, *I* was the person judging whether their justifications made sense.)

Just as on my language arts final essay, I could have influenced student responses on the final assessment by giving a practice assessment first, scoring it together, and then giving a nearly identical assessment to be used for my report-out. Had I been asked for the student papers to verify my data, there would have been nothing amiss about them. They would have been taken at face value because there was no evidence to the contrary. That is not what happened, but given the fact that it *could* have been, I wonder how many teachers across the district opted to influence their report-outs in a similar way.

Once Morris signed off on my goal scores, it was a mystery how they were computed in the total. I had to trust that the new system worked because there was no recourse available to me if I suspected it did not.

As these goals became a fixture in our evaluation psyche, teachers came to realize that the worse their baseline scores, the better their growth would be. Many teachers began giving the baseline assessments on the first day of school, even joking about it as we prepared for each school year during orientation week. Is this practice what the CDE and district officials envisioned teachers would gravitate toward?

Probably not, just as they did not envision teachers might 'manage' the growth they reported in ways that worked to their advantage. It seemed odd to me that, as a sixth-grade team, we never discussed the goals we had chosen or how our students were progressing on them across the school year. With the enforced "collaboration" on so many other things, the fact that this was completely ignored in faculty meetings surprised me. I now wonder if it was part of the union stipulation that a teacher's goals must remain private.

The table on the next page, which also appears on page 92, was shared with us by our principal in August 2013. We were told to use this chart as a reference for the raw score we received based on the pie chart distribution of points. If we landed in the white area two years in a row, we would be put on probation and monitored closely by our principal for two years.

Educator Effectiveness Matrix				
Compare this table with the raw score on your final evaluation to determine your overall rating.				
Highly Effective				
Effective				
Partially Effective				
Ineffective				
	0-12.5	12.6-25	25.1-37	37.1-50

I never landed in the white or light gray area, even though Morris gave me numerous partially effective ratings on the Quality Standards (see page 122) for three years in a row, from 2013 to 2016.

In August 2014, we were informed that if our rating fell in the black or dark gray area, we would be awarded a one-time bonus, in addition to the Cost-of-Living Adjustment (COLA). If it fell in the light gray or white area, we would be awarded only the COLA.

The growth goals became routine, and as the years went by, they grew in significance. By 2018, Individual Educator Goals had become 30% of the evaluation while the evaluator's review of professional practices was still 50%.[7]

So…80% of our performance-based evaluation relied on unverified (and unverifiable) data.

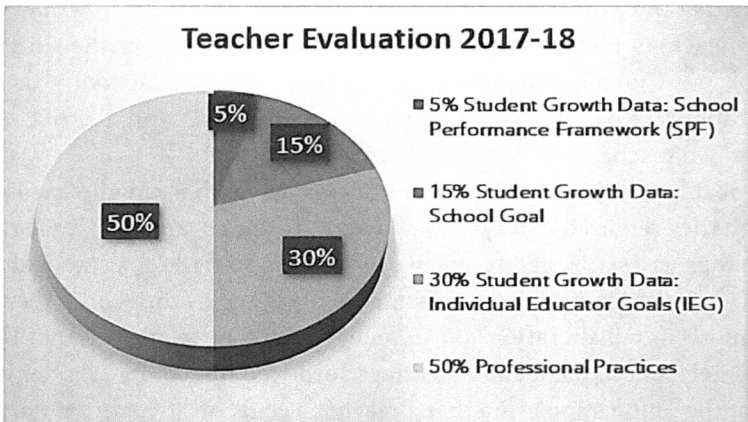

Teacher Evaluation 2017-18

- 5% Student Growth Data: School Performance Framework (SPF)
- 15% Student Growth Data: School Goal
- 30% Student Growth Data: Individual Educator Goals (IEG)
- 50% Professional Practices

Student Growth Data: School Performance Framework (5%) and **Student Growth Data: School Goal (15%)**, in the diagram above, fulfill the requirement of "collective attribution" in SB 10-191.

---

[7] Current research shows that the new Colorado State Model Evaluation System has adjusted the final effectiveness composition to 70% Professional Practices and 30% Measures of Student Outcomes: https://www.cde.state.co.us/educatoreffectiveness/faqs

Ramifications

The reason I share so much of this is to show what happens when politicians enact mandates without considering the realistic implementation of them. The document I shared is rife with complexity, and you saw less than a fifth of this 21-page packet. All this just to write *goals*!

If Colorado's General Assembly *did* consider the implementation of their legislation, understanding that such a wordy and involved scheme would be created because of it, that is an even more disturbing thought: the elites believe there is nothing wrong with turning education into a convoluted web. [8]

The new evaluation system seemed like a slap in the face, but even more alarming is how it was presented to us, as if it were a perfectly reasonable solution to lagging student performance. (Based on the test scores I shared on page 45, it's a wonder this law hasn't actually been repealed yet.)

The bottom line is that school districts were handed an ill-advised mandate and charged with meeting its requirements. If you read through the stipulations for setting our growth goals, you may have noticed this paragraph on page 94:

> **Teachers:** State statute and rules specify that teachers, or licensed personnel with direct instructional responsibilities, must set goals that pertain directly to gains in student learning in reference to the Colorado Academic Standards...

The requirement to *"set goals that pertain directly to gains in student learning"* is a weak attempt on the General Assembly's part to hold teachers accountable for the performance of their students. For one thing, it's nearly impossible to design a functional process for creating these goals, given the limitations placed on school districts by the teachers' unions. The way my district handled it appears to be an example of giving in to union demand that loopholes and caveats be allowed upon *implementation*.

It is time to face and defeat the real monster in education.

There are other ways to assess how a teacher is performing that involve actual transparency, [9] but school districts have long been constrained by the

---

[8] Remember this idea when you read chapter 13, The Search for Transparency.
[9] See chapter 18, Our Model School.

demands of the teachers' unions, which do not exist to protect the integrity of public education, despite the rhetoric they routinely spew. They exist to propagate their own power and bottom line. I sat in union meetings for two years as a representative for my school, between 2001 and 2003. After that, I was inspired to withdraw my membership. [10]

Throughout that first year of implementing these goals, I wondered how the public would react if they understood how SB 10-191 was implemented at the school level. What sane person would think it's a good idea to have a teacher report her own growth data that directly affects her job status and salary? Not only did our principal tell us she didn't want us to turn in the assessments that back up the data, she and her assistant principals never even asked to *see* them.

Consider, also, the deceptive spin of telling teachers that the new evaluation system gives them control over their own evaluation. The only control exists, potentially, in the self-reported data, encouraging teachers to grab at that potential to the extent of committing fraud.

And then there are those Quality Standards that must be used to evaluate educator performance. Way back on page 2 of this book, you can see the CDE's requirement in the second bullet point:

- Evaluation based on statewide Quality Standards defining what it means to be an effective teacher, principal/assistant principal, or special service provider; the professional practice Quality Standards account for half of an educator's annual evaluation.

Those standards are interpreted and applied by *one* person, with credence assigned to his findings as if he is an actual measuring instrument. It boggles my mind that anyone believes this process could ever be completely objective. But maybe no one in authority actually does believe that. Maybe they all understand that this law simply pays lip service to the *idea* that Colorado now has a "performance-based" teacher evaluation system. And maybe they hope they'll be able to con the public for years to come so that those tax dollars for education administration will only continue to grow.

SB 10-191 is a legislative boondoggle. [11] And it will never work as advertised for the simple reason that the teachers' unions run the show. These unions

---

[10] You can read more about my experiences as a union rep on page 206.
[11] Boondoggle: work or activity that is wasteful or pointless but gives the appearance of having value. *Source: Oxford Languages, Google's English Dictionary.* https://languages.oup.com/google-dictionary-en/

fought tooth and nail to defeat the passage of this bill, but once it became law, their tactics shifted to how they could mitigate the new evaluation systems to the benefit of their members, something they have been extremely successful at. With all the loopholes and caveats that are surely available in any of the evaluation systems across the state, the only thing that would make union members happier is if they could return to the pre-2012 way of doing things.

Meeting one's students for the first time is exciting and occasionally unnerving... Discovering you may have been set-up adds a whole 'nother dimension....

10 A Smack in the Head

In August 2013, as I was preparing for the new school year, I walked into the teachers' break room for lunch, carrying my new roster with the intent of quizzing my fifth-grade colleagues.

"So," I said, setting the roster in the middle of the table where they were eating. "What can you tell me about these students?"

This was a typical exercise by the sixth-grade teachers; we shared a wing with the fifth graders, and it was considered a good idea to get a heads-up about the class dynamics we were looking at for the year. Jane picked up the paper first and after a moment, let out a disdainful sigh. [1]

"My God," she said, "it's like we never made class lists last spring." She shook her head at me, and I thought, *Well, it can't be that bad, can it?*

"Nick and Monica. Together again," Jane continued, handing the list to Karen. "I feel sorry for you, TerryLynn."

"Why?"

Karen answered me. "Neither of them has a filter. They say whatever's in their head, all the time. And they often choose each other as a target."

"What's their academic status?" I asked. Beside each name, I saw the letter *H*, which (in our jargon) means 'high performance or aptitude'.

"They're both very bright," Jane admitted. "But they won't conform to classroom expectations, and that makes them difficult to teach."

I nodded, pondering that.

Karen said, "Even if you can manage to work with Nick and Monica, you'll have trouble with Kiernan. He is a pain in the neck and loves it." She let out a big sigh. "And his mom is even worse." Before I could ask the question, she continued, "And, yes, he is also bright."

---

[1] Not her real name. The names of colleagues have been changed to protect their privacy.

I smiled.

"But stubborn," she continued. "See if you can get him to follow *any* rule."

"What's so bad about him?" I asked. "Other than the rules."

"He picks on kids," Karen said. "Under the radar. And his mother backs him up. *Her* little darling could *never* do anything bad."

Christine took the paper from Karen. "Oh! You have Aaron Ingram, too," she said.

"What's wrong with him?"

"He's real...emotional," she said. "Doesn't follow direction. Doesn't do most of his work. Has a tendency to bolt when he's upset."

"Bolt?" I asked.

"Run out of the room."

"To where?" This came from my sixth-grade colleague, Chris, who was looking amused.

"Sometimes the bathroom. Sometimes Doc's office. Sometimes the hallway overlooking the gym." Christine shook her head as if in painful memory.

Susan was next. She looked at the paper and smiled. "You have Candace Abrams. She is definitely GT. You'll love her."

"What are her behavior issues?" I asked warily.

"None. She's a sweetheart. And you can put her with anyone to work." I thought about that. "But you also have Jackie Clark."

"What's Jackie's issue?" I asked.

"He doesn't want to be in school," Susan said, smiling. "He spent all last year lobbying his parents to let him home school."

"And?" I prompted.

"Obviously, it didn't work. But he thought that the worse his grades were, the more likely they were to cave. He's very capable, which is why we didn't retain him. He can do the work, and even more, if he wants to."

I resolved to inspire him to want to.

"And there's one more thing," Susan said. "He's Kiernan's best friend."

I spent a lot of time planning how to work with my new crew of students, knowing that I had some tough personalities to deal with. I felt like I was up to the task, especially since most of the behavior issues were also GT, or near, material.

When our Meet and Greet night occurred later that orientation week, a time when our students come to school for an hour to meet their teacher and get a locker assignment, I thought that perhaps my fifth-grade colleagues had overstated their case. Maybe a summer of growth had helped, but I didn't see any poor behaviors, or even a hint. Nick courteously accepted his bottom locker assignment, even though the top lockers are usually the coveted ones. I didn't want him towering over anyone, knowing that he might be a bit of a sticky wicket in the hallway.

Monica had come to school sans parents, which partially defeated the purpose of Meet and Greet. We give our parent base the forms they must fill out and sign before we will assign a locker, so that's usually the incentive to be present. Monica had flitted in like a butterfly and giggled at me that she couldn't get her mom off the couch to come to the meeting. I couldn't help smiling at that. I had told her she could take the forms home to be filled out and bring them back on Monday. I also gave her a top locker, partly because she was a head taller than any other student. To her credit, Monica brought all her papers back, properly filled out and signed, on Monday morning.

Kiernan was the only student who seemed as if he thought he was 'too cool for school'. His mother carried his backpack of supplies and did all the talking, even though I addressed all my questions to him. He kept tossing his over-long blonde bangs out of his face and looking at other students speculatively. It was my policy to allow students to choose their own desk at first while I summed up personalities in the first week of school. I steered Kiernan, however, toward a side desk by the window with the explanation that his height might make it difficult for those behind him to see. He acquiesced pleasantly, almost defying his mother to object.

While nothing had stood out to me negatively during the Meet and Greet, it became clear during the first week of school that the mix of personalities in my room was anything but serene. They fed off each other in the most inane ways, often creating havoc where not a hint of it should have been. Fifth grade colleagues chuckled in sympathy when they saw my crew "lined" up outside, kicking, pinching, and annoying each other. Christine confided that she had cautioned Rebecca strenuously against putting Darin in the same room with Jackie or Kiernan, and against putting Monica with Nick. She couldn't imagine what admin had been thinking when they made up my roster.

After a few weeks with my student load that year, it became easy for me to believe the fifth-and sixth-grade scuttlebutt: I had been targeted this year, for reasons I did not understand. Or maybe I did. [2]

---

[2] These students served as the models for the student characters in my novel *Finishing School*.

Prior to 2012, I was considered among the most competent teachers in the fifth and sixth grades in my school. Colleagues routinely came to me when they needed teaching advice or help penning a letter to a parent. I received excellent reviews on performance from my principal, who enjoyed evaluating me herself rather than assigning me to one of her assistant principals.

In the fall of 2012, however, I suffered a head injury in our school hallway. I'm sure Gary Morris, the administrator in charge on that afternoon, considered it my fault because I was not watching where I was going when I plunged head-first into a 4-inch steel girder. He may even have convinced Rebecca that I faked the injury. The district sent me to a behavioral psychologist to be assessed. (The psychologist told me that I wouldn't have faked an injury using symptoms experienced by only 2% of concussion victims.)

The effect of slamming my head into a solid object was devastating; my ability to manage my classroom was seriously impacted that year, and the damage re-emerged at various times thereafter, with snippets continuing to this day. My Workmen's Comp doctor continued to prescribe half-time teaching for a period of three months after the accident, something Rebecca complained about bitterly. At one point, she marched into my room after school and demanded to know how long I was going to 'require' a half-time substitute.

Rebecca also ignored her own requirement to observe my teaching, writing on my year-end evaluation that there had been some confusion surrounding whom I had been assigned to, so observations of performance would not be included.

The next school year, I found myself handed off to assistant principal Gary Morris for evaluation. Thus began three years of being labeled partially effective in many areas of my performance review.

Blindsided

In early November 2013, a year after my accident, I was called to Gary Morris's office after school. He had just completed his third observation in my classroom. I thought it would be a short meeting to point out some strategies he wanted me to use and send me on my way.

It was short. That part I got correct. I was not prepared for the preliminary evaluation he handed to me, however, when I sat down.

"This is what your final eval will look like if things don't improve," he told me.

I stared at the document. Over and over, I saw 'partially effective' written next to indicators:

- Implements research-based best practices in instruction;
- Develops lesson plans incorporating effective lesson design;
- Models and facilitates higher-level thinking, problem solving, creativity, and flexibility;
- Adapts instruction to meet the instructional needs of all students;
- Provides varied opportunities for student demonstrations of learning;
- Explicitly communicates criteria for student success;
- Provides meaningful and constructive feedback to students;
- Develops and carries out appropriate consequences in the classroom.
- Maximizes available instructional time.

I was stunned. How could this be? I had never had a poor rating as a teacher. It seemed impossible that I could be facing one now. Additionally, I had been given no previous warning that things were stacking up this bad. It is part of an administrator's job to let teachers know immediately if they are seeing anything questionable. *And* to do it in a way that seems designed to help, not demoralize.

Morris then reminded me that his assessment of my teaching made up half my evaluation. If I couldn't convince him to change his marks on those indicators, I would be rated *partially effective* or *ineffective* at the end of the school year. Those findings are not audited by anyone. Yet they can put someone on probation or end their career.

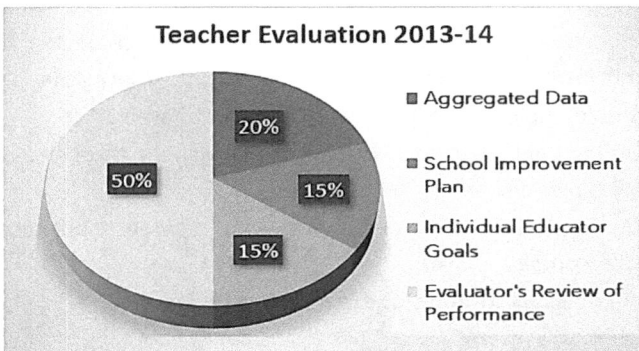

Teacher Evaluation 2013-14

20%	■ Aggregated Data
50%	■ School Improvement Plan
15%	▨ Individual Educator Goals
15%	▨ Evaluator's Review of Performance

I was devasted and immediately thought of asking Rebecca to be transferred to her for evaluation. (The other assistant principal was not an option because he oversaw grades K-4.) Then I realized that just the request would mark me unfavorably. Additionally, it didn't seem plausible that Rebecca herself was not in on the plan to ruin me.

After that dismal meeting, I spoke with the other assistant principal in our building anyway. I asked him if he would come to my room to do an official observation of my teaching. He regretfully informed me that he could not; it would be seen as a violation of professional courtesy. Since he was not assigned as my evaluator, he felt it was inappropriate to over-step his bounds. Besides, he was the rookie administrator in the building. I knew what that meant.

"You're kidding!" my colleague Mary had exclaimed, sitting in my room, watching me examine the pre-eval in near tears. "It couldn't have been that bad."

"It was awful," I assured her, handing the paper over. "Here. Read it yourself."

"You're partially effective at *maximizing available instructional time*?" she said. "That's pretty lame."

I nodded, depressed.

"It's also very subjective," she had mused. "What are you going to do?"

"I don't know," I had said. "I don't think there's anything I *can* do."

Later that evening, I sat and stewed over the preliminary eval. Why was Morris so down on me? Showing up for three observations couldn't possibly have given him a definitive picture. To write such a horrible review only two months into the year just seemed malicious. Then it occurred to me to examine the *other* indicators, those that Morris *had* deemed effective:

- Demonstrates accurate, up-to-date knowledge of subject;
- Demonstrates knowledge of how to integrate subject matter/disciplines and literacy across content areas;
- Plans and implements district-adopted curriculum through alignment of resources and assessments;
- Aligns content within course and with previous and succeeding grades/courses;
- Communicates to students expectations for learning;

- Uses a variety of formative and summative assessments to make instructional decisions;
- Develops relationships with students that fosters a culturally responsive learning environment;
- Collaboratively develops, models, and communicates clear expectations for student behavior within a learning environment;
- Implements classroom and building rules and procedures;
- Participates in professional learning opportunities and applies what is learned;
- Establishes and maintains professional communication which is clear, responsible, and respectful;
- Establishes and maintains meaningful two-way communication in a timely manner with students and guardians;
- Collaborates to accomplish team, school-wide, and district-wide goals and practices;
- Maintains up-to-date records of student progress according to District policy and school norms.

How could he know any of *this*, either? He had never asked me how I *'collaboratively develop, model, and communicate clear expectations for student behavior within a learning environment'*, yet he marked me effective at it.

I might have expected to be labeled partially effective at *'Collaborates to accomplish team, school-wide, and district-wide goals and practices'* and *'Participates in professional learning opportunities and applies what is learned'*, given my participation in professional development and team meetings, yet he had marked me effective on those, also. Additionally, there is no way he could know whether I *'plan and implement district-adopted curriculum through alignment of resources and assessments'*, since he'd never seen an assessment I had given or asked what resources I used.

The idea that I could be partially effective at *'explicitly communicating criteria for student success'* yet effective at *'communicating to students expectations for learning'* also made little sense. It seemed that Morris had rolled the dice to determine which standards to ding me on.

The more I thought about those Quality Standards, the more they seemed to be a list of meaningless Edu-speak designed merely for appeasement of people higher up in the food chain. [3] Each of them could

---

[3] You can see the full list of standards on page 122 or in Appendix A, page 216.

be interpreted in whatever way the principal wanted, yet everyone treated them as if they were not only an authentic measuring tool, but also biblical in stature.

Being in favor had been a wonderful thing, and these standards had never represented anything of consequence, let alone malice. Now that the principal's ratings had actual bite, the standards could be used against me at the whim of my evaluator and his boss, with no recourse available to me.

> This is why people should be concerned about teacher evaluation schemes. They all rely heavily on the subjectivity of one person while being labeled "performance".

I limped through the rest of that year and managed to 'earn' an evaluation that showed *partially effective* on only three of the standards. I did not end up in the white area on the Matrix of Evaluation. The biggest effect this experience had on me was that I was always on edge after November 2013, particularly when Gary Morris was around.

Does anyone think this is what the framers of SB 10-191 had in mind? Just as they expected that teachers would implement growth goals with fidelity and a desire to improve their practice, they surely hoped administrators would use the Quality Standards to support rather than imperil teachers.

Systems like this must be abolished.

But read on for what I experienced when I *was* in favor.

As yet...no one knows the exact formula for success in teaching. The complexity of personality and the many-sidedness of teaching have continually baffled useful analysis.[4]

Many people both inside and outside of education question whether current systems are valid or whether they work at all to ensure effective teaching. After all, principals may see as little as 0.1% of instruction if they observe one teaching period per year based on 5 periods per day and 180 school days a year. Bump that to observing 3 periods per year and that's still only 0.3% of teaching, leaving many to wonder...

What happens in the classroom the other 99.7% of the time?[5]

---

[4] Frederic Butterfield Knight, 1922. From the source listed below.
[5] Robinson, Sheila B. From Frontline Education): "Teacher Evaluation: Why It Matters and How We Can Do Better". Quote attributed to Marshall, K., "It's Time to Rethink Teacher Supervision and Evaluation." *Phi Delta Kappan*, Vol. 86, No. 10, June 2005

11 The Spin Game

Necessary Evil

Before SB 10-191, *teachers* were *evaluated*. We *did* have to set goals and we *were* rated on our performance in the classroom.

But it was such a silly enterprise that I'm surprised any of us got through it without laughing at the absurdity of it. We all knew that once we reached non-probationary status, it would take a major misstep on our part to receive any unsavory consequences.

I saw evaluation as a necessary evil to appease those above us who thought we had an easy job. It may help to note that I was in favor with both the principal who hired me in 1998 and her successor until 2012. My biggest worry was setting up my observations so I could shine in my very best light, which I always did. I found it fun to perform for my principal, but the truth is, what I did in front of her was very like what I did every day , anyway. I often forgot she was in the room, in fact, because I was so caught up in the delivery of my lesson.

There was a lot of paperwork to be done by our supervisors, however, which does take away from running a school effectively. How can this type of bureaucracy possibly be useful? In hindsight, I believe *that* evaluation process was a way to accumulate documents for due process if a teacher was deemed worthy of involuntary transfer.

If you want a little fun some time, compose an email to your district's superintendent asking him what the process is for involuntary transfers in his schools, including how many occur per year, and copy the School Board president. For extra laughs, copy a prominent writer at your city's newspaper.

Teacher evaluations prior to SB 10-191 were a laughable enterprise. They had no backbone and were not taken seriously by teachers. We sat through our required year-end conferences with the principal and nodded politely as she discussed her "findings" with us. If those findings were particularly wonderful, we did a lot of smiling and joking.

The facade even then, however, was that the narratives our principal wrote about us and how she marked us on the Indicators of Performance represented valid measurement. School systems have long adhered to the idea that a teacher's performance can be accurately assessed by one person coming into a classroom to observe a lesson a few times a year.

Really? *One* person, with no one to audit his findings, is entrusted to rate our teaching performance as if he is both an expert and an automaton. Does anyone seriously think this is probable? I don't. Final evaluations are subject to the *spin* the evaluator wishes to attach to the observations he has made.

Here is an example: Say a teacher puts her desks in rows because her students have proven they cannot or will not work together meaningfully. The principal who comes into her classroom to officially observe her teaching notices this and writes on his notes *'Student desks placed in rows. This discourages collaboration in learning. Not a best practice.'*

He could as easily have written *'Student desks placed in rows due to behavioral concerns. Teacher appears to be experimenting with ways to gain student trust and cooperation, a best practice.'*

If the student desks are placed in table groups, the principal might write *'Student desks placed in table groups for collaboration, following best practices.'* He could also write *'Students encouraged to be off-task due to desk placement.'*

Gary Morris *did* write me up for having my desks in rows that school year of 2013-14. My students were so unruly that the most I could do to encourage collaboration without anarchy was to put my rows in twos, so that students had a discussion partner right next to them. I was responding to the maturity and cooperation levels of my students, and I explained that to Morris. He refused to concede that I might have a point, and that since I was in the room all the time with my students, my view of reality might contain more validity than his.

Principals can spin their performance observations any way they want with impunity. **There is no auditing of a principal's findings on performance,** yet this process has been a time-honored tradition in our schools for decades.

The point of this book is not to encourage a return to our pre-2012 evaluations. They were as pointless as the current system, designed to mollify officials who needed the appearance of an evaluation system.

Grain of Salt

Before 2013, my evaluator was not Gary Morris. It was usually Rebecca, our principal. She always loved observing my teaching and discussing it afterward. I also enjoyed the process. As I look through my folders of evaluations for the first fourteen years of my Colorado career, I see many positive narratives about my classroom performance, such as this one from 2007.

> "A masterful teacher, Terry[Lynn] continues to bring humor and a sense of meaningful purpose to all learning opportunities within her 6th grade language arts block. On a daily basis, Terry[Lynn]'s students get a hefty dose of rapid-fire instruction designed for student growth and success. While some such practices might create high levels of stress among students, Terry[Lynn]'s signature playful banter and her keen sense of who can be pushed to higher order thinking through an analysis or evaluative question and who requires expertly scaffolded questioning techniques to reach similar heights of engagement, foster superior performances among her students. This along with well established routines, structures for each segment of instruction and expectations make for an optimal instructional practice that assures that learning transpires." [1]

This favorable narrative, based on Rebecca's pre-arranged observations at three different points of the school year, continues with more praise for my ability to question students expertly.

For all she knew, I was a total monster the rest of the time. And even if I wasn't, maybe I was simply putting assignments on the board and distributing worksheets. How can three observations verify that I was a "masterful teacher"? [2] This is why principal ratings of teachers should be taken with a grain of salt.

---

[1] I have all the original documents to corroborate the narratives contained in these evaluations.
[2] By contract, the principal was not allowed to include any information that had not been gleaned through an official observation of performance.

The evaluation that contains this narrative is what we called the short form, a single page observation verification used for those non-probationary teachers who were in a non-evaluation year. At the top was a *Statement of Purpose*, sharing that Colorado law *did* require professional staff to be observed annually, even when not in our "required evaluation cycle".

Every three years, a non-probationary teacher was considered to be in an evaluation year and was put through the 'long form', a more exhaustive piece of work containing 11 pages of narratives and ratings on that teacher's performance.

The sample below is a narrative from page 2 of my long form evaluation from 2008:

"In preparation for this year's teaching assignment, Terry[Lynn] examined last year's student performance data. <u>She discovered that there were some gaps, chiefly in the area of writing, between females and males (97% and 91%, respectively).</u> This realization <u>prompted a goal to bring the gap within 2% points.</u> Her intervention strategies included: communicate <u>a clear expectation, provide written feedback, target through instruction any weak performance areas related to state standards, and track progress prior to this year's CSAP.</u> These strategies are simply, but most significantly, <u>the mark of a thoughtful, reflective and attentive teacher.</u> All of which are strong characteristics of Terry[Lynn]'s teaching practice."

You may have noticed that I've <u>underlined certain sentences.</u> I feel like I should add some clarity, because the spin on this piece of writing is incredible:

a) "<u>She discovered that there were some gaps, chiefly in the area of writing, between females and males (97% and 91%, respectively)</u>": This statement makes it seem as if it was my own idea, independently, to examine the student performance data. It was not. This came from the orientation session in August, when the sixth-grade teachers were handed our CSAP data from the previous year and guided toward noticing what our principal wanted us to notice. If we failed to do so, she pointed it out herself, in this case, the gap between female and male writing statistics.

b) "This realization <u>prompted a goal to bring the gap within 2% points</u>": The principal suggested to our entire sixth grade team that we work on decreasing that gap for this school year. We asked if 2% would work and she said yes.

c) "Her intervention strategies included: communicate a clear expectation, provide written feedback, target through instruction any weak performance areas related to state standards, and track progress prior to this year's CSAP": These were not my intervention strategies; they can be found in an intervention manual and were probably discussed in one of the team meetings that our instructional coach attended, at the behest of her boss, the principal.

d) "These strategies are simply, but most significantly, the mark of a thoughtful, reflective and attentive teacher": At the time, I was gratified to be in our principal's good graces to the point that she wanted to embellish how I planned for and worked with my students. Imagine, though, how these remarks might have been written had I *not* been in favor. She could easily have written that I was resistant to the data that was obviously in front of me, and that without her to point it out, I would have ignored a key piece of evidence. And it would have been technically accurate.

Additionally, her final paragraph might have been spun against me, without dishonesty. Here is what she actually wrote:

"Ms. Zempel believes that 6th graders do best in their acquisition and application of language arts skills when the material is suited to them developmentally (i.e., shorter texts rather than longer works – novels) ... Her use of the literature anthology as a sole means of instruction reflects this impressively."

She might have written this as a criticism instead, saying that I used only one source for reading instruction, the literature anthology textbook, rather than bringing multiple sources, including full-length novels, into my instruction. She could even have slanted her words to indicate that I was ignoring best practices by teaching only from the textbook, which was actually not true. I included many supplemental materials in my instruction, but since Rebecca had not written the above words as a negative toward my teaching, I did not refute them at the time.

While I was glad to receive such great evaluations, I wish it had occurred to me to ponder the significance of using praise as a vehicle to rate teachers. What purpose did it serve? And what purpose does it continue to serve? Even with the new evaluation systems created in response to SB 10-191, principals are still able to use praise, validly, in their evaluations of teachers.

As you read the following narrative from a different long form, 2005, try to see how it contains anything of substance:

"On November 30, 2005, Ms. Zempel's students were completing a vocabulary drill on words from Unit 6. As students participated, Ms. Zempel commented on the quality of their answers and used her signature sense of humor to encourage students to actively participate. Her clever banter cultivated an atmosphere of fun and excitement with a lesson that might otherwise have been dull."

These narratives **count as performance based.** How? Every bit is subjective, just like the ratings principals assign each teacher regarding the Quality Standards I have already mentioned several times in this book. While that list for our district varied slightly from year to year, overall, it maintained a similarity of requirements.

Here are those Quality Standards from 2013:

Professional Preparation

a) Demonstrates accurate, up-to-date knowledge of subject matter.
b) Demonstrates knowledge of how to integrate subject matter and literacy across content areas.
c) Implements research-based best practices in instruction.
d) Develops lesson plans incorporating effective lesson design.
e) Plans and implements district-adopted curriculum through alignment of resources and assessments.
f) Aligns content within course and with previous and succeeding grades/courses.

Professional Responsibilities

a) Participates in professional learning opportunities and applies what is learned.
b) Establishes and maintains professional communication, which is clear, responsible, and respectful.
c) Establishes and maintains meaningful two-way communication in a timely manner with students and guardians.
d) Collaborates to accomplish team, school, and district goals and practices.
e) Maintains up-to-date records of student progress according to District policy and school norms.

Professional Practices

a) Communicates to students expectations for learning.
b) Models and facilitates higher-level thinking, problem-solving, creativity, and flexibility.
c) Adapts instruction to meet the instructional needs of all students.
d) Administers all building, District, and State assessments with fidelity.
e) Provides varied opportunities for student demonstration of learning.
f) Provides meaningful and constructive feedback to students.
g) Uses a variety of formative and summative assessments to make instructional decisions.
h) Explicitly communicates criteria for student success.
i) Develops a safe and welcoming learning environment.
j) Develops relationships with students that foster a culturally responsive learning environment.
k) Collaboratively develops, models, and communicates clear expectations for student behavior within a learning environment.
l) Develops and carries out appropriate consequences in the classroom.
m) Maximizes available instructional time
n) Implements classroom and building rules and procedures.

As you look over these standards, try to imagine how feasible it would be for a principal to know, definitively, how a teacher is performing on any of them. (It wasn't then, and it isn't now.)

Our principal rated us on them every three years, however, after we passed the initial three-year probationary period. In addition, we had to choose three to set as specific goals for ourselves. We didn't *do* anything with these goals; they were merely part of the going-through-the-motions routine, just like observations of instruction. Rebecca would ask me, during our end-of-year conference, to share how I thought I'd done on each of the goals I had picked, and I'd spend about five minutes saying things like, 'I think it went well this year. I found some things on the internet to support what I was doing, and I feel good about the outcome.'

Softball stuff, if you ask me. (Perhaps you can see why the new eval based on SB 10-191 was such a shocker to all of us in 2012.)

Evaluation systems of teachers at that time existed merely to appease those in charge. They had no real value and no one in education took them seriously. Teachers and principals went through the motions in a sort of choreographed dance with each other. You could say we understood the drill.

By law, we had to be monitored in some way. Providing the big bosses at the CDE with a list of Quality Standards was the key to keeping them out of our schools and classrooms. Only the bad teachers (those who did not instruct so much as assign) had anything to worry about, and even that was nothing to get too upset over. Receiving a poor evaluation did mean the loss of your job (once you had reached tenure), but it did affect your reputation and your ability to remain in a school where you enjoyed teaching or to voluntarily transfer to another school.

By the way, we did have to set data goals during our pre-eval conference with our principal in September. They were related to CSAP scores from the previous school year; here are mine from my 2005 evaluation:

ACTION PLAN FOR GROWTH		
Writing:	Baseline:	89% Adv/Prof. on CSAP
	Goal:	92% Adv/Prof. on CSAP
Reading:	Baseline:	94% Adv/Prof. on CSAP
	Goal:	96% Adv/Prof. on CSAP

Nowhere in the next year's evaluation were the results of these goals mentioned.

In a growth mindset, people believe that their most basic abilities can be developed through dedication and hard work—brains and talent are just the starting point.
This view creates a love of learning and a resilience that is essential for great accomplishment. [3]

[3] Dweck, Carol. 2015, from *Renaissance.com*: https://www.renaissance.com/edwords/growth-mindset/

12 Why Growth?

Education in Colorado pushed its way to the forefront of legislative consideration in 2000 when the first statewide CSAP scores were published. [1] The range of proficiency outcomes rose to 100% in one school but plummeted to 6% in another ... *in the same district.* A disparity like this causes hand wringing at the highest levels in government.

The angst was exacerbated by the uncertainties created by *No Child Left Behind* (NCLB), signed into law in 2001. Provisions under this law "set new federal expectations for school performance and introduced financial consequences for chronic substandard outcomes." [2]

Michael Watson, a former principal turned consultant, has criticized NCLB for what he calls a 'blind spot':

> [NCLB] did little to measure students' actual academic growth. By punishing and rewarding schools on the basis of a narrow definition of proficiency — whether their students were mastering grade-level content — the law neglected other key indicators of student learning, such [as] how much progress students were making on other standards. As a result, the entire educational ecosystem, including classroom instruction, was oriented around a single and very limited measure of student performance...
>
> ... As a teacher and principal, I saw firsthand how these narrow state assessments failed to reflect the complete picture of how much or how little our students were learning. [3]

---

[1] DenverPost.com: 4th Grade Reading CSAP Scores. 2000
[2] Watson, Michael. "Student Growth Measures: What we've been missing." 2019
[3] Ibid.

While Watson applauded NCLB for shedding light on a glaring need for improvement in both standards and accountability, he also wrote that the new law missed the mark in meeting the needs of students *"where they are."*

On its surface, this sentiment makes sense: if a child enters fourth grade reading at a first-grade level but manages to improve to a third-grade level by the end of the year, that's a significant gain. However, that child will likely score at the unsatisfactory or partially proficient level on his state test because he still cannot comprehend the grade level questions on it.

Watson has consistently pointed out that this unsavory outcome prevents us from seeing the whole picture. Testing vehicles are just not created to give comprehensive information about our students. They are configured to provide information about a narrow view of achievement.

He's not the only one who experienced discontent. The sentiment against NCLB's insistence on proficiency-only as the arbiter of success rankled many education experts in the years between 2002 and 2008. In 2009, stakeholder meetings were held across the nation to determine how to modify NCLB: the overwhelming opinion was that *growth* should figure into the equation.

Lawmakers then wrote their follow-up to NCLB, the Every Student Succeeds Act (ESSA), another euphemistically titled mandate that modified its predecessor "by directing states to **capture student 'growth** or another valid or reliable measure' as part of the accountability systems." [4]

Already saddled with continuing discontent over CSAP scores, Colorado's lawmakers decided to comply with ESSA by mandating a massive overhaul of educator evaluation across the state. By 2011, they had written their new bill and used their own euphemistic spin to get it passed at the state level in Denver. [5] News leaked out to school districts much like gossip in a small town. I remember hearing rumblings from assistant principal Rose Keebler with a sense of denial.

Once SB 10-191 became law, it also became a subject of curiosity regarding its impetus and aftereffects, leading to multiple analyses by interested onlookers. One such study was conducted by Sarah Melvoin Bridich for her graduate dissertation at the University of Denver. I find the following part of her introduction provocative (but not surprising), particularly the sentences I have typed in bold:

---

[4] Watson, 2019, and U.S. Department of Education: *Every Students Succeeds Act.* www.ed.gov/laws-and-policy/laws-preschool-grade-12-education/every-student-succeeds-act-essa.

[5] SB 10-191: *The Great Teachers and Leaders Act.* Enacted into law Nov 2011.

Recent research supports a direct link between teacher quality and student learning. At the same time, it is argued that the current teacher evaluation systems are not working. **Under current teacher evaluations, most teachers are rated as exceptional. Yet students perform far below the exceptional level on state, national and international assessments**. Although numerous factors contribute to student performance on said assessments, **there appears to be a disconnect in the dichotomy between teacher ratings and student performance that is problematic**. Precisely which elements of teaching lead to improved student learning and how to measure those elements remains unclear. [6]

This disconnect between teacher ratings and student outcomes must have been disconcerting to Colorado's lawmakers. I am equally sure they didn't know how to address it as they contemplated drafting their bill. Perhaps they were overthinking it. Or maybe their status as outsiders to the profession prevented them from seeing the big picture: *principals and teachers work very closely together and must, as a necessity, build collegial bonds with one another*. Without those bonds, a schism develops between what is desired from instruction and what is delivered to students. When the new evaluation requirements were unveiled, that schism became unavoidable, as principals were now viewed as adversarial rather than collegial. [7]

When I wrote on page 123 that *"teachers and principals went through the motions [of evaluation] in a sort of choreographed dance with each other"*, I was referring to these collegial bonds that outside researchers cannot possibly understand. If our principal and one of her teachers did not click, that teacher would not last long in our school. The teacher would transfer out of her own accord, with the blessing of the principal.

Bridich, an outsider to education, wrote her dissertation *"in partial fulfillment of the requirements for the degree of doctor of philosophy."* [8] It is useful to read theses such as hers because they help illustrate the divide between education research conducted by even well-meaning outsiders and the people who then must live with the decisions often derived from that research. [9]

---

[6] Bridich, Sarah Melvoin. "Perceptions Surrounding the Implementation of Colorado Senate Bill 10-191's New Teacher Evaluation." 2013.
[7] See chapter 18, Our Model School, for my plan to eliminate this unfavorable outcome.
[8] Bridich, S. "Perceptions…" title page.
[9] You can read more analysis of Bridich's paper at
 https://www.schoolmattersfoundation.org/history-behind-sb-10-191

Make no mistake; education legislation is not met with favor by the educators who must implement it. Proponents of that legislation try to sway public opinion by insisting this is because teachers must now do the job they were hired to do, without a union to protect their lazy and/or incompetent backsides. The reality behind the reticence, however, is that most legislation paves the way for top heavy, ineffective policies like the teacher evaluation system handed down by my district in 2012.

The urge to reform teacher evaluations has deep roots. We can trace discontent back to 1983, when the newly formed Department of Education published *A Nation at Risk*, a document that fomented for years before leading to the boondoggle of mandates in the 2000's. [10] The fact that it took nearly 20 years for NCLB to begin this wave is a testament to the power of the teachers' unions, organizations that I wholly do not support.

In fact, an ironic truth is that while these unions claim to uphold public education as a critical component for the education of our youth, their machinations are the primary reason our teachers are saddled with pointless requirements and our schools are failing.

A parallel truth is that more than twenty years after NCLB, legislation continues to be *unable to circumvent* union power.

A common thread among education experts and policymakers is the belief that teacher activity is the primary contributor to student success. Ms. Bridich mentions this frequently in her paper; prominent researchers like Hattie and Tomlinson are overt in their own assertions, as well. As an offshoot of this sentiment, then, it seems natural that teacher evaluations and student outcomes should be irrevocably welded to each other. NCLB, however, offered no realistic avenue toward achieving this. When ESSA granted permission to use a growth measurement to rate learning, a pathway suddenly opened.

There was still a roadblock, however.

When we veer toward using test scores (in *any* sense) as a measurement of teacher performance, we wander dangerously close to butting heads with the teachers' unions, who wield tremendous power in setting public education policy. **Care had to be taken to create evaluations that could rely on growth but not on test scores.** [11]

---

[10] *A Nation at Risk: The Imperative for Educational Reform.* 1983

[11] The inappropriate use of test scores as a way to measure teacher performance is perhaps the only common ground I share with the teachers' unions. See chapter 18, Our Model School, for my plan to evaluate teaching.

An emphasis on *growth* in student learning had been a best practices buzz phrase for years, advanced by the studies of Stanford psychologist Carol Dweck, who coined the term *Growth Mindset*. We studied the growth mindset as a way to improve our metacognitive teaching and help kids understand that their achievements are not predetermined.

How the Growth Mindset works:

> In studies that examine mindset, participants are given statements such as: "You have a certain amount of intelligence, and you really can't do much to change it." Participants who disagree with such statements are considered to have more of a growth mindset. However, agreeing with such a statement would mean that the participant has more of a fixed mindset. [12]

Carol Dweck has been known as the leading researcher in growth mindset for 30 years. In her TED talk, "*The Power of Believing You Can Improve*", she explains how a growth mindset "leads to a focus on learning, increased effort, and a willingness to learn from mistakes." [13]

That willingness to learn from mistakes is an essential component to education. If students do not experience failure, they cannot process their mistakes and grow from them.

One way to help students develop a growth mindset as opposed to a fixed mindset ("I'm not good at math; I just don't get it") is to provide **meaningful feedback**. In 2014, we studied a handout provided by The National Center for Women & Information Technology. [14]

8 Ways to Provide Effective Feedback

1. Explain that mental effort actually changes the brain and increases its capacity.
2. Tests and assignments do not assess the student's ability or potential.
3. Focus feedback on student progress, strategy, persistence, and effort.
4. Recognize that preparation and ability are not the same thing.
5. Feedback should offer specific guidance on how to change.
6. Do not lower standards for success.
7. "Wise feedback" is particularly important when pointing out missteps.
8. Always offer the opportunity to discuss your feedback.

---

[12] "Growth Mindset". *Psychology Today.*
[13] From TED: Ideas Worth Spreading. Carol Dweck -The power of believing you can improve.
[14] NCWIT: 8 Ways to Give Students More Effective Feedback Using A Growth Mindset

Many of these points are not only valid, but crucial in developing a growth mindset, such as helping students understand the difference between *preparation* and *ability* (point four). However, look again at the second point. This could be a confusing and misleading thing to tell children. I think I see where the authors are going with it, but it does need clarification. On its surface, it appears to tell students that there really is no purpose for tests and assignments, and I'm sure that's not the intent.

Jane E. Pollack, a colleague of Dr. Tomlinson at ASCD, penned an article titled **How Feedback Leads to Engagement**, which we also read and dissected in 2014. She wrote, in part:

> Previous learning models, influenced by behaviorism, viewed the student's role in the feedback process as passively waiting to receive feedback from a teacher, while newer neurological research shows that humans biologically anticipate and seek feedback. In a classroom, feedback can be more powerful when a teacher gives students opportunities to seek and receive feedback. [15]

A significant takeaway is that student growth is more likely to occur **when students are held accountable for taking the initiative in their learning.**

Pollack recommends providing reflection templates to students, so they can record their metacognitive thoughts about each lesson. A form such as this might be used:

Date	Goal	Pre self-observation: what I know; what I don't know, etc.	Post self-observation: what I learned; how I learned it; what I still need to know	Level of effort I put into my learning

The teacher supplies only the date and the lesson goal. Students fill in the rest, before the lesson and again afterward as a reflection of their learning. The teacher reviews the chart and discusses it with the student. This discussion is what creates the 'meaningful' part of the feedback; however, in order to *be* meaningful, discussion must occur immediately upon student

---

[15] Pollack, Jane E. "How Feedback Leads to Engagement", 2012.

completion and teacher review of the form. Can you imagine doing this with 30 students every day? Even if it only takes 2 minutes per student (not likely unless one is content to have a superficial conversation only), that's an hour away from instruction. An hour for just sitting around while one waits for his turn with the teacher. And during that time, the teacher (of course) is not teaching.

Dweck and Pollack have proposed excellent ideas for working with children, as have Tomlinson from chapter 2 with her ideas on differentiation and even John Hattie from chapter 3 with his visible learning. The trouble with relying on research that has not been analyzed adequately and realistically, however, is that you often end up with faulty legislation that does not work as intended. [16]

It does appear that politicians and district officials allow themselves to be influenced by articles that appear in education journals, such as this one from *Renaissance.com*:

Why compare growth:

Proficiency is measured at a single point in time, and the benchmark is the same for every student. In contrast, growth is measured at points over time and reflects progress among those points in time. The static benchmark is replaced by a specific score within a dynamic range of growth—typical, less than typical and greater than typical growth. Because growth compares students to their academic peers, it is possible that a student who falls short of proficiency is actually growing at a typical, or higher than typical, rate. The same could be said for students who ace the proficiency yet fail to grow at a typical rate.

This article goes on to describe two case studies advancing the idea of growth as a better measure of a child's success than proficiency:

Doug is in third grade, but he starts the school year reading at a first-grade level. He is not meeting benchmarks. Throughout the fall and winter, his teacher creates an intensive reading practice intervention plan for him. By spring, he scores at a second grade reading level. Although Doug is still not proficient his scores indicate that tremendous growth has occurred.

Simone is also in third grade. She starts the year reading at a fourth-grade level. By spring, she again scores at the fourth grade reading level. Although Simone has flown by benchmarks, she is not growing. Her

---

[16] These excellent ideas fall short when teachers try performing them in packed classrooms. See chapter 18 for my idea on making class sizes and teacher/student ratios productive.

teacher makes an effort to keep Simone moving along an accelerated path for reading practice. [17]

What's missing from the second scenario is that Simone's class placement might be faulty. Instead of being in a general ed classroom, she could benefit from being placed with students who are also advanced readers, taught by a teacher who has shown expertise at developing higher level reading prowess.

Unfortunately, when authority figures read articles like this, where there are only two case studies presented, there is a real possibility of forgetting that 28 other students also occupy this classroom. Tasking one teacher to differentiate for substantial growth in every one of them is like asking one engineer to design all the plumbing and lighting in the Chrysler Building.

Latching onto research like this without considering the full picture of what goes on in a classroom has not, in my opinion, served our lawmakers well.

It is clear that everyone at the top of the food chain wished to find the panacea for lagging student success. Encouraging an emphasis on growth is not a bad idea; in fact, it makes a lot of sense if combined with an expectation for achievement and the recognition of merit, *and* if the onus for it is laid at the learners' feet.

It makes *no* sense, however, to combine student growth with teacher evaluation. If that doesn't mesh with your own thinking yet, perhaps you should re-read how my district set up measuring growth in our classrooms on pages 94– 102.

While everyone *wants* improvement, very few people in the upper echelons of education policy understand (or would even support) that realistic reforms cannot focus on only one leg of a three-legged stool. It is disheartening to read about the eagerness with which reformists championed their cause in 2000 when their efforts didn't even come close to panning out as envisioned:

> Two decades ago, the national conversation about how to improve our public education system was full of energy and new ideas. Policy makers across the political spectrum were eager to adopt reforms that would raise the quality of the American educational experience while boosting student outcomes and ensuring our kids would remain competitive in what was then an already globalizing economy. [18]

---

[17] Betebenner, D. W. "Growth". 2009.
[18] Watson, 2019.

This is largely due to ignoring the responsibility of the other legs on that stool. And because of that, the third leg has done everything possible to protect itself from perceived injury. As a result, we are no closer to resolving the issue of lagging student achievement than we were in 2000.

Regrettably, the way politicians have managed education reform over the last twenty-five years reveals a woeful ignorance of human nature:

> When nothing is riding on an outcome, an individual is not likely to value that outcome. When everything is riding on an outcome, an individual is likely to maneuver the outcome to his advantage.

Bureaucracies are inherently antidemocratic.
Bureaucrats derive their power from their position
in the structure, not from their relations with the people
they are supposed to serve. [19]

- Alan Keyes

---

[19] Keyes, Alan, American politician. Quote taken from www.**BrainyQuote.com**

13 The Search for Transparency

I hope you will view this book as a starter for your own research. Find out for yourself what your state values in its teachers and what legislation it has passed regarding education. Do an online search for critiques of that legislation. [1]

Investigate what your state board of education has mandated as a teaching doctrine. If it involves performance-based evaluation systems, find out the nuts and bolts of that. Peruse both the state's website and your own school district's to find out how teachers are evaluated. If this search takes longer than twenty minutes and you still find nothing definitive, put your state representative and school board on the hot seat. Ask questions. Try to find out what's going on behind the Edu-speak.

This is a menu on the home page of the Colorado Department of Education's website: [2]

> -Educator Licensing
> -Colorado Performance Management System
> (RANDA)
> -Educator Preparation
> -ESSA Requirements for High Quality Teachers
> -Log into Colorado Licensing (COOL)
> -Jobs for Teachers
> -Principal Resources
> -Professional Educator License Renewal Requirements

---

[1] All links and information shared in this chapter were valid as of Jan 2025.
[2] https://www.cde.state.co.us/

I decided to click **Educator Licensing** first and was not surprised when I was taken to a page with a multitude of requirements, but nothing that spoke to evaluation. So I returned to the home page and clicked the second link, **Colorado Performance Management System** (RANDA).

Here is part of what you get when you click that link:

About

The Colorado State Model Performance Management System (COPMS) in RANDA is an optional tool to support districts in the implementation, data collection and effective use of the Colorado State Model Performance Management System. The Colorado State Model Performance Management System was available to use beginning with the 2014-2015 school year.

Finding nothing that I considered useful, I again returned to the home page and clicked on the third link, **Educator Preparation**. These are the choices from the right side of that landing page:

Educator Talent Home
Educator Preparation
Educator Effectiveness
Educator and Leadership Development
Educator Career Navigation
Research and Impact
Educator Talent Newsletter
Contact Us [3]

I clicked the fourth option, Educator Effectiveness. Scrolling down a little, I found a green bar labeled **Educator Evaluation 101**.[4] I clicked it and was taken to a page that gives an *Overview of Educator Evaluation* in Colorado. Scrolling down, I saw buttons for learning more about the *State Model Evaluation System, Local Model Evaluation Systems, Senate Bill 10- 191*, and *Senate Bill 22-070*. Scrolling down further, I saw this link: Rubric for Evaluating Colorado Teachers.[5] I clicked it and was taken to a nine-page pdf document

---

[3] https://www.cde.state.co.us/educatoreffectiveness/copms. This landing page has been altered slightly from previous versions of it.
[4] https://www.cde.state.co.us/educatoreffectiveness
[5] https://www.cde.state.co.us/educatoreffectiveness/revised-teacher-rubric

filled with tables of information about how three quality standards are evaluated:

I. Mastery of pedagogical expertise in the content taught.
II. Establishing a safe, inclusive, and respectful environment for a diverse population of students.
III. Planning and delivering effective instruction.

If you haven't been following along on the internet with the links I've shared, it might be worthwhile to do so now. You'll see that each webpage is filled with Edu-speak: lots of information that sounds so complex, this could be a website for SpaceX. (Except that Elon Musk is known for simplifying processes rather than making them unnecessarily convoluted.)

Think about what teaching *should* be: working with children and training them to become effective readers, writers, and mathematicians. If we can do that, they will become effective self-learners. Why is it any more complicated than that? If you have explored the CDE's website further than the pages I've already mentioned, you may come to the same conclusion as I: the elites want us to think education is too complex for any of us to understand. And the more they pack their websites with Edu-speak, the easier it is to disguise agendas that include equity, diversity, and indoctrination.

Continuing my exploration, I decided to look at the websites of all the school districts in the Denver metro area, beginning with Denver Public Schools. On their home page, I clicked **Menu** and saw these choices at the top of a long string of others: About DPS, Superintendent, and Board of Education. This is in huge contrast to what welcomed me when I went onto their home page in 2022:

> COVID-19 Dashboard
> Information About Vaccines
> COVID-19 Guidance
> Headlines
> Trans Day of Remembrance
> DPS Unveils District's First Electric Bus
> Announcing DPS Land Acknowledgement
> Transgender Awareness Week: Parent Testimonials

While the new look is an improvement over the previous one, I still did not see any options for *Teacher Evaluation* or *Curriculum*. This information should be included at the very top of the menu, along with Live Feed, News,

Events, and Documents, which you have to scroll down to find on the home page.

If you click Board of Education from the home menu, you will be taken to a page with lots of blue buttons, including a Contact button.[6] Clicking that will provide email links to contact each member. Clicking the Meetings button takes you to a page with a Meeting Schedule and instructions about how to sign up to make a *Public Comment* at the meeting. Here are some of the requirements:

- No more than 30 minutes for any "action item" *(whatever that means)* will be devoted to public comments.
- No speaker may have more than two minutes to make his point.
- No one may speak twice. *(I can only conclude that this means 'ever'.)*

My overall impression about speaking at a board meeting is that the option is extremely limited and very regulated. And one more thing: the school board has established different levels of meetings, some of which are held in secret, as noted below.

Meeting Types

Regular meetings are held on the third Thursday of each month at 4:30 p.m., unless otherwise noted. The board votes on each month's action items during this meeting. Regular Board meetings are held at the Emily Griffith Campus, 1860 Lincoln St., Denver.

You are invited to attend our meetings in-person and/or watch them through our video streaming files. Please notify the Board of Education Office at least 48 hours prior to the meeting of any special accommodations.

Work sessions are held on the first Thursday of each month, unless otherwise noted. These meetings serve as an opportunity to prepare for the regular meetings and to study issues before voting.

Public Comment is held on the Monday prior to regular meetings.

Executive session is when the board may recess from a board meeting to a closed session for discussion. Topics to be discussed are limited to matters under the law such as personnel, real estate acquisitions, security or consultation with attorneys. All executive sessions are closed to the public. Board members may not vote during executive sessions.[7]

---

[6] https://www.dpsk12.org/page/board-of-education
[7] https://www.dpsk12.org/o/dps/page/board-meetings

What I could glean from the menu option Board Meetings is that what I wrote about them originally in 2022 is the same as what's available currently, with the caveat that public comment is now allowed in person. In 2022, board *meetings* were held in person, but public comment occurred online: you had to join via Zoom and wait to be unmuted when it was your turn to speak. You had three minutes before being re-muted. Today, public comments have been trimmed down to two minutes per speaker.

Back to my quest: I had now spent more than 30 minutes perusing this website without seeing any links for curriculum documents or teacher evaluation, so I clicked on the Search box in the upper right and typed in *curriculum*. That took me to a page with links to curricular articles about individual schools, but I did not find a document that delineates what is taught at each grade level. I *did* see a button below the search results labeled Documents. Clicking it, I was taken to a page where I saw this:[8]

Documents

doc	**How Curriculum, Assessment, and Instruction Work Together**

File size: 801 KB   Date uploaded: Apr 30, 2025

/documents/Assessment / Assessments / Reading to Ensure Academic Development Act (READ A/15435601

Research, Analytics, Assessment & Data

When I clicked *that* link, I landed on a two-page pdf document explaining how curriculum, assessment, and instruction work together. One sentence in the second paragraph on the first page caught my attention: *"Schools are encouraged to use assessment to inform instruction, not to drive instruction."* [9] Further explanation of that seems very much like either splitting hairs or using the technique of doublespeak that I first mentioned on page 1:

> This means that teachers should use assessment results to understand the areas of growth for their students. Assessment is not the end result,

---

[8] This link was updated on April 30, 2025. The original link I accessed had been posted on Nov 7, 2023. The document is identical to that originally uploaded.
[9] DPS Document: How Curriculum, Assessment, and Instruction Work

but a way to measure whether students have mastered the necessary skills for success in college and career.

Additionally, the blurb about *Item Teaching* sounds like a kid trying to justify that copying his spelling assignment from his neighbor is not *really* cheating because he was thinking about the spelling words as he wrote, so his brain *was* learning something from the copying.

It's disingenuous:

District leadership, via this document, suggests that schools should avoid tailoring their instruction to what is tested (Item Teaching, or 'teaching to the test') because that *"denies students the opportunity to engage in a rich, college-preparatory program* [and] *prevents* [them] *from learning critical skills for success."* However, providing instruction for anything that is *not* tested means less attention to what *is* tested, and every teacher knows that the results of those tests are of paramount importance to the Department of Education (and by extension, to DPS itself). The district also knows this, so their cautions about *'teaching to the test'* seem insincere.

After this brief rabbit-hole excursion, I returned to the Home Page of DPS, where I scrolled all the way to the footer to see what might be hidden down there. I discovered a link to Literary Curriculum Transparency and thought I had hit paydirt. When I clicked it, however, I was taken back to the CDE's website, where I read more Edu-speak about Colorado's initiative to *"require each local education provider to submit the following information to the department of education and requires the department to post the information on its website"* (SB 21-151):

- The evidence-based or scientifically based core and supplemental reading curriculum, or a detailed description of the reading curriculum, by grade, used at each of the schools operated by the local education provider.
- The targeted, evidence-based or scientifically based core and supplemental reading instructional programs and intervention reading instruction, services, and other supports, or a detailed description of the programs, services, and other supports provided by each of the schools operated by the local education provider.
- The number of students enrolled in kindergarten, first, second, and third grades who have READ plans, as well as the number of students who have achieved reading competency.

- The local education provider's budget and narrative explanation for the use of the "Colorado READ Act" intervention money. [10]

On page 89, I wrote about the three stages of overhauling our perceptions of teaching, with stage one being "*convince us that our job was more complex than we had previously thought.*" This strategy appears to be directed at the public, as well, given the information and wording I've found so far at both the state and district levels.

The final search I made in my multi-hour perusal of Denver Public Schools' website was for its mission and vision statements. I found them under About DPS on the main menu. Here is the mission statement, and from the wording, it says a lot about the chaos in our schools:

Educational equity is our collective responsibility. We prepare students for career, college, and life. We create conditions and partnerships where students, families and team members belong and thrive. [11]

This mission statement says nothing about learning or achievement. It's all about experiences and inclusion. This may seem innocuous, but it portends a lack of emphasis on skills or merit.

If you keep reading, you see this:

...we want to continue transforming Denver Public Schools into a school district grounded in equity. This districtwide focus on equity will be embedded in everything we do, so that we can help break historical patterns and become a school district that is designed to inspire every student to dream big and make their own future.

This is, again, doublespeak. Public schools have *always* had the mission of inspiring students to dream big and make their own future. The word *equity*, however, negates this. **Equity means individual effort is not required to turn dreams into reality.** The fact is, *equity* is a misunderstood concept: it means an *equal outcome*, something that cannot be guaranteed unless we do away with personal responsibility. Because the word sounds so similar to *equality*, people assume that *equity in education* means 'equal opportunities for all'. Not so. There are two words for a reason. This webpage, and indeed, the entire website, are filled with misleading language designed to appease, and even mislead, a public that wants a great deal from its tax-supported

---

[10] https://www.cde.state.co.us/coloradoliteracy/literacycurriculumtransparency
[11] https://www.dpsk12.org/page/mission-and-vision

education. It is our responsibility to analyze that language to find the reality behind the words.

Continuing my quest, I spent an additional hour and a half trying to find teacher evaluation information and curriculum documents on four more Denver metro school district websites, eventually admitting defeat. This information should be readily available to taxpayers and parents, without a struggle to locate it. There should be a link on the home page of every school district for these three items: **Teacher Evaluation Protocols, Budget for Evaluation**, and **Curriculum Documents**. *(Perhaps I would add statistics for each school regarding transfer requests. This tells you a lot about the quality of leadership in that school.)*

Instead, there is a lot of jargon that seems like it's only there to make the average person feel stupid and lose interest in finding out more about their school district. The education elite have apparently concluded that the more they portray education as being too sophisticated for the rest of us to understand, the more we will give them *carte blanche* to perpetrate their wasteful and disingenuous schemes.

The most useful item I happened upon in my original 2022 search is that my former district suspended teacher evaluations for the school year 2020-2021, for obvious reasons, I would think. I'm sure the teachers were doing cartwheels about it. [12]

Let's return to the information about DPS's school board, shared on page 140. If you wish to attend a meeting, you supposedly can do so, either in person or through live streaming. However, when I followed the links for DPS's new **Diligent Community**, starting at the Board of Education's home page, I was not successful in actually streaming the archival footage of a meeting.[13] Through this fruitless search, however, I did find out more about Public Comment. [14]

From the May 1, 2025, agenda, the first item (1.01) describes new protocols for allowing public comment, including that any speaker **must have an established relationship with DPS**. This relationship can take many forms, including being a DPS employee, a parent or guardian of a student, or a resident of Denver, to name a few. While this requirement may seem

---

[12] You can read my op-ed about the COVID shutdown of schools at
https://www.schoolmattersfoundation.org/
[13] https://dpsk12.community.highbond.com/Portal/
[14] https://www.dpsk12.org/o/dps/page/board-meetings

reasonable on its surface, further reflection should spawn some questions. One that immediately comes to *my* mind is *How does DPS receive its funding?* If that funding comes from any public source outside Denver, then the restriction to allow only Denver residents to speak at a board meeting is an unacceptable one. (I found the answer to that question by asking Google where Denver Public Schools gets its funding and received a quick response from Generative AI.)

School districts and their governing boards should be *required* to open their meetings (and speaking opportunities) to anyone who pays into their system or has a stake in it (e.g. parents, employees, *and* taxpayers). They should also be compelled to live stream every meeting, and to make access to that stream and the archival footage of it easy to obtain.

School districts receive billions, each year, in taxpayer monies; they should not be allowed to operate as a private entity, where we, the public can be told, "It's not your business." *Or*, to make it so difficult to obtain information that most of us will simply give up out of fatigue or frustration.

It's time to look seriously and without bias at the monopoly on taxpayer funding that public schools enjoy. They know they are going to receive that money regardless of what they do. *(The published budget for DPS this year is $1.45 billion. [15])*

Politicians who enacted NCLB and ESSA may think they dramatically reduced the power of school districts to act as private entities with doublespeak as their primary avenue of communication, but they are wrong. Their legislation barely put a dent in it. This is not to say that more federal legislation is the answer. No, *less* federal legislation in the form of a repeal of both laws would be a start in the right direction. Follow that with common sense modifications to state legislation, based on the understanding that *less* is *more*, and we're one step closer to cleaning up the chaos.

Finally, abolishing the federal department of education is a necessary step toward eliminating the circular bureaucracy that has ensnared all of us. If you want a taste of the Edu-speak that dominates *that* department, visit *their* website: https://www.ed.gov/.

---

[15] https://www.dpsk12.org/o/dps/page/superintendent

What can we do individually to repair our broken schools?

Become an activist at the level of your comfort. At the very least, you should ask your local school board what ratio of adult to students in each classroom exists in your district, and how class sizes are determined. Your follow-up question should be *"How much of your budget is spent on evaluating teachers, and what does that evaluation look like?"* Additionally, if you cannot find curriculum documents that delineate, specifically, what is taught at each grade level, ask for them. Also ask why they're not published to the website.

These questions can be addressed in an email to the individual members of the school board; in fact, if you put all their addresses on the same email, they will know that you are serious about answers. If you copy that email to the superintendent and several prominent journalists in your city, you will really get their attention.

If you have a child who attends a public school, make sure the secretaries know who you are. No need to be obnoxious; just be visible. Attend parent meetings; ask why fundraising is necessary and how the funds are spent; ask for the rationale for whatever grading system is used; ask how many teachers requested a transfer last year; ask what system is used to evaluate teachers and why it is used. Finally, ask to visit the classrooms unannounced.

If your school principal demurs on any of these items, consider that a problem.

Teacher Recruitment and Salary

Recruitment is an aspect of teaching that most people probably don't think about. The interview process is a farce. And it is controlled by the unions. You would think that in an important field like education, those doing the hiring would be able to ask whatever comes to mind in order to get to the heart of what a candidate has to offer.

Not so. The procedure is heavily scripted by the district under the direction of the union. In my former school, the principal convened a committee comprised of the teachers who teach the same grade level and perhaps another administrator or counselor. Here is the procedure we followed, designed to elicit nothing of substance from the candidate:

- Choose from a set of pre-approved questions, all of which are suggested by the district and union.
- Set up interviews, one after the other, for a stretch of three to five hours after school. Each interview must last the same amount of time. Ours were 30 minutes. A timekeeper on the committee is assigned.
- Prior to the interview, the candidate is given the set of questions to prepare while she waits.

The agreement with the union is that the candidate must have the questions *15 minutes prior* to the scheduled interview. That means she can jot down her ideas beforehand. If she has guessed the content of many of the questions (not difficult, because every interview committee chooses from the same list of approved questions), she has probably already done an internet search of great answers for questions about philosophy of education, best practices in instruction and discipline, and familiarity with popular teaching programs.

It is not permitted to ask the candidate any question that she has not been given beforehand. How is this an authentic process? It is also not permitted to ask follow-up questions other than, "Can you say more about that?"

In my experience, it is impossible to tell how good a teacher might be from the interview. Anyone can put on a good show, and the candidate who is the most persuasive and strikes a positive chord with the principal is the one who gets the job. The committee turns out to be for show only, as it fulfills an agreement between the district and the union.

How would I change the hiring process? I would conduct it in two stages:

First, ask questions that pertain to the specific job, such as an opening for kindergarten or sixth grade or eighth grade science. (These questions can be standardized so that every candidate for kindergarten, for instance, receives the same questions to start off. Follow-up questions based on answers provided by the candidate will likely differ.)

Also, ask questions that are perhaps unexpected, such as *'What is the most difficult teaching situation you have experienced?'* or *'What would you do if you didn't get along with someone on your team and it appeared they were out to get you?'* I would also ask new questions inspired by previous responses from the candidate.

Asking questions about education theory or learning platforms elicits nothing of substance. Every candidate who has ever taught (or attended any teacher prep program) knows these questions and answers intimately. The information they share is a waste of everyone's time. If the candidate has made it to the interview table, he has a transcript that assures us he knows what teaching is. **What we want to know is how he will handle teaching**. The interview should be videotaped for later perusal by the committee. It will be useful to cross-reference his responses with how the candidate conducts himself in stage two of the process and throughout his probationary period.

The most important part of the interview stage is that the candidate will not be given the questions ahead of time.

Second, watch the candidate teach a lesson. Prep the students beforehand to behave as naturally as possible and not be overly cooperative. Some might even be coached to be difficult, such as asking why they must learn this material, playing with a toy at their desk, or even just not participating.

When a job offer is made, it will be with the understanding that if the new hire turns out *not* to be a good fit for the position, he will be terminated, with a generous severance package.

I'm sure my ideas for hiring teachers would be problematic for the unions, but you know what? The unions are problematic for children. When you read about my model school in chapter 18, apply these hiring practices. I think they would be better at staffing a school than the current useless scheme.

The salary schedule for teachers is another nonsensical thing. The concept of a guaranteed income, regardless of the value one adds to a program, is a hallmark of the teachers' union. It may sound like a good idea, but the minute we venture into the realm of equity in our compensation of teachers, we begin to absolve them of being good at their job.

Here is part of the 2023-24 salary schedule for Denver Public Schools:

Years of experience	B.A.	B.A. + 18 graduate credits	B.A + 36 or M.A.	M.A + 18	M.A + 36	M.A + 54
STEP	Level 1	Level 2	Level 3	Level 4	Level 5	Level 6
1	$54,141	$56,514	$59,472	$62,695	$65,921	$69,146
2	55,395	58,480	61,437	64,738	67,963	71,189
3	57,230	60,447	63,402	66,780	70,006	73,229
4	59,066	62,413	65,369	68,823	72,047	75,272
5	60,904	64,378	67,335	70,866	74,091	77,316
6	62,737	66,345	69,301	72,906	76,132	79,357
7	64,575	68,311	71,268	74,951	78,117	81,400
8	66,409	90,275	73,233	76,994	80,217	83,443

This chart continues to Step 20, with a BA worth $88,000 and an MA+54 graduate credits worth almost $108,000. [16] The vertical steps refer to years of teaching experience. Each year, a teacher moves downward one step on the pay scale. The level is the amount of education a teacher has. As you can see, it behooves one financially to have education beyond a bachelor's degree.

Once new teachers realize this, they begin working on those magical post-graduate credits so they can enhance their salary as quickly as possible. The usual method is to take online classes from some institution. My district paired up with Adams State University in Alamosa, Colorado, to offer online courses that could get you to Level 2 without much effort. The courses offered were taught by school district personnel and were often quite lightweight, involving a lot of 'discussion' threads. A grade of 'A' was easy if you 'said' lots of positive, party-line things in your 'discussions'.

You only had to work seriously at a graduate program if you wanted that master's degree, but it still could be achieved completely online. Once that was in place, you could return to the casual method of taking lightweight online courses to add to it. In fact, it is possible to get to an MA+54 without taking a serious course of study leading to a PhD.

If you *do* have a doctorate, you will gross more than $72,000 in your first year of teaching and nearly $118,000 by your 20th. This means that if you worked in the State Department with a PhD to your name and decided to retire from that high-stress job (with a nice pension), you could then start a second career in education, making more money in your first year of teaching than a veteran teacher with 10 years' experience. But think about this: a first-year teacher is not an expert at teaching, regardless of how many post-graduate degrees she holds. How is she worth $18,000 more per year than her B.A. counterpart?

Further support that advanced degrees mean nothing on their own:
- If you have a post-graduate degree, it doesn't matter what your field of study was. Only that you have one. How does an M.A. in Art History ensure that one will be good at teaching first graders how to read?
- A second-career teacher with an M.A. in sociology will make more money in her first year of teaching than a B.A.-only teacher in her fourth year of service. If that sociologist-turned-teacher adds more

---

[16] https://thecommons.dpsk12.org. This is a website designed for employees or potential employees. Perusing it was very interesting. Unfortunately, as of August 2025, it is no longer available to non-employees. The 2024-25 salary schedule, with an increase of over $1,000 at each Level, is currently available via Amazon through an internet search.

graduate credits, she will continue to widen the gap between her own salary and anyone with less 'education' than she, regardless of how she handles herself in a classroom.

- A beginning teacher with a master's degree in education but no experience working with children will make more money than a B.A.-only teacher who has three years' experience. One also doesn't have to prove any prowess in order to get the salary to go with that degree. After coming to New Mexico, I taught with a teacher who had an M.A. in computer library media, yet didn't know how to set up a document camera, use the cloud, or save files to a thumb drive. I know, because she asked for my help.
- By 2023, 54% of Colorado's teachers held M.A.'s, [17] yet fewer than 40% of third graders in Colorado could read proficiently. [18]

When teachers are consumed with a mission to get as many post-graduate credits as they can for the single purpose of moving right on the salary schedule, it competes with what should be our primary purpose: instructing children.

How does all that graduate school make one a better *teacher*, particularly at the elementary level? New teachers, regardless of their age or education, spend their first two years just getting their feet on the ground; there is no way they are experts right off the bat.

Level of education does not necessarily improve quality of instruction. Experience does that. *And* collaborating with other teachers. *And* watching demonstration videos. **But the best indicator of quality teaching is the temperament of the teacher.** The tenacity she is willing to put toward helping her students learn using winning strategies is invaluable. The successful teacher not only persists daily in the struggle to get students to achieve but also exhibits a great deal of patience. Graduate school does not ensure any of this.

So why do school districts reward what they *know* doesn't help children learn? Because it looks good on paper. And school districts are on a perpetual PR mission. If you're not convinced of that, go onto DPS's home page and look at their self-advertising at the top, with their "thanks" to the taxpayers for passing their 2024 Bond. [19]

---

[17] National Center for Education Statistics; accessed through Generative AI, 15 Feb 2025.
[18] https://www.cde.state.co.us/assessment/2023_cmas_ela_math_
Statesummaryachievementresults
[19] https://www.dpsk.12.org/. Unfortunately, this message has since been removed.

Anyone with two years of college can become a valuable adult in an elementary classroom. The internet is a vast resource, after all. If the salaries in the table I shared were averaged across the Levels of Education and based only on years of experience, *and* if we hired and retained only teachers who have demonstrated they can teach, we could fix a lot of the mess we're in right now. [20]

As you might imagine, this idea falls flat with the M.A. teachers. And the unions. But ask yourself why that might be.

---

[20] See chapter 18, Our Model School, for my plan.

Bureaucracy:

A system for controlling or managing...

an organization that is operated by a large number of officials employed to follow rules carefully. [21]

---

14 Testing, Part Two

Prior to current PARCC-style state testing, many districts evaluated student learning using the ITBS, [1] an assessment I remember from my own childhood. If you haven't looked at this test lately, it might be worth your time now. [2] The questions on it are mostly multiple choice, such as this one for proofreading:

> Find the mistake in the following passage:
>   A.   During the noisy soccer game,
>   B.   my dad got a headache we still
>   C.   had fun anyway.
>   D.   (No mistakes) [3]

In my opinion, this is a good question because it gets straight to the point of whether students understand basic sentence structure or not.

Here's another question, this time for reading comprehension:

> Lucy was no ordinary girl. She had been born with a special gift, a gift other people considered to be unusual. When she was only 3 years old, her parents noticed she had a special way with animals. She loved animals and the animals that she came into contact with were especially attracted to Lucy.
>   Why do Lucy's parents think she is different from other girls?
>   A.   She talks to animals.
>   B.   She likes to go to the zoo.
>   C.   She has a special gift.
>   D.   She does not have any friends. [4]

---

[1] ITBS: Iowa Tests of Basic Skills
[2] https://www.tests.com/practice/Iowa-Test-of-Basic-Skills-ITBS-Practice-Test
[3] https://mercerpublishing.com/iowa-assessments/sample-questions
[4] Ibid.

This is also a worthwhile question because a correct answer indicates that a child has carefully read and understood the paragraph. The word *'animals'* appears several times, but the correct answer *(C)* does not contain that word at all. (By the way, this question is a variation on asking *'What is the main idea?* [5])

Here's an ITBS 3rd/4th grade question about pattern logic: [6]

Which of these figures doesn't belong?

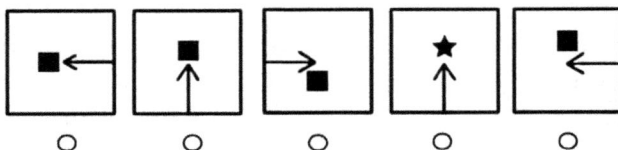

And a 5th grade question on calculating area: [7]

Consider the U-shaped figure below, which has dimensions given in cm.

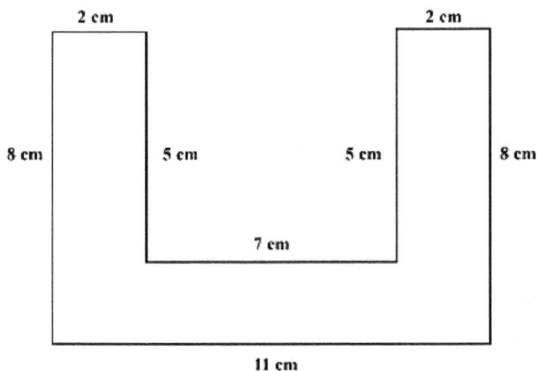

What is the area of the U-shaped figure? Enter just the number. Do not put "cm", "squared", or anything else.

---

[5] https://mercerpublishing.com/iowa-assessments/sample-questions
[6] https://www.testingmom.com/tests/itbs-test/
[7] https://www.test-guide.com/quizzes/iowa-5th-grade-math-practice-test

Compare this area question with the one on pages 51 and 52. Both questions require the student to understand what area is and how to calculate it. But which one requires non-math skills in order to get a perfect mark on it?

Here's the $64,000 question: **Just what are we testing** with the PARCC-style tests that 18 of our states are using? Or the Common Core-influenced tests that 45 of our states are using? Are we testing math prowess... or *keyboarding* skills and how to navigate an online testing program correctly...?

I encourage you to explore the three practice test websites cited in the footnotes on the previous page. They represent plenty of rigor, yet they're all either multiple choice or fill-in-the-blank. When we give this type of test, we come closer to accurately assessing the way a child's brain thinks because our assessment is not stymied by a child's inability to type in a text box.

Could the area question on pages 51 and 52 be rewritten as a multiple-choice question rather than a *'show your work and explain it in the text box'* question? Sure.

But state officials often worry that on tests like that, where students do not share their ideas in writing, they are merely regurgitating facts rather than assimilating and analyzing them. Does the area question on the opposite page look like it requires mere regurgitation?

I would suggest that any state giving the PARCC test also give the ITBS and then compare results. If there's a significant difference in outcomes, perhaps one of the tests is assessing things other than what it claims.

Beginning in 1997, ITBS in Colorado was slowly replaced by the Colorado Student Assessment Program, officially mandated in 1993 by the legislature when it ordered the Colorado Department of Education to develop both a list of standards and an assessment tool. The first test was rolled out in 1997 to 4th graders only. By 2001, students in grades 3-7 plus 10 were taking the reading and math tests. [8]

Colorado's CSAP began as a booklet test that students wrote in. It contained multiple choice and short answer questions, plus at least one essay prompt for the English Language Arts booklets. For the math booklets, students showed their work in boxes and often had to explain what they had done on the lines provided below the boxes. When children wrote their answers in pencil like this, most of them spent a lot of time on their responses.

---

[8] See the entire timeline of Colorado Testing in an article by Nic Garcia at *Chalkbeat Colorado*. 2017. See link in *References*, p. 224.

Once typing became the norm, that ceased to be the case. There should be a correlation here that someone at the state level surely has noticed. Why it is given no credence is a mystery. The requirement to type in text boxes *must* be affecting student responses on these very involved tests.[9] This is what I alluded to on page 58. If I were designing testing for an elementary school, I would return to the use of test booklets with handwritten responses. I am certain that would provide a more accurate picture of student achievement.

Until 2012, CSAP data was not overly emphasized in our school, by either the principal who hired me or her successor. Maybe that's because our scores were usually above 85% proficient.

In August that year, however, Rebecca (who took over as principal in 2005) handed us our CSAP data for the previous *three* years, telling us to study the growth or regression from one year to the next so we could make some correlations.

I noticed a see-saw effect: the second year showed a decline over the first year, followed by an increase in the third year. Analyzing scores like this didn't make much sense to me because they represented different groups of children taking the tests, something I mentioned when Rebecca stopped at our table to listen in. I said I thought it was like comparing apples to oranges. In addition, I pointed out that the scores didn't necessarily represent what our students *could* do; they only showed what students *cared to do* on that specific test day. There are many reasons a child might perform poorly on any given day of his life: ill health, a fight with mom, forgetting his lunch at home, a particularly lazy day. Many times, testing motivation is out of our control.

This comment was not well received by our principal, who insisted that we *could* improve our students' performance on CSAP if we walked around the classroom enough and stopped pointedly at the desk of any student who appeared to be loafing around. I thought a more effective way of engendering investment would have been to give students and their parents a presentation about how test results would be used to assign children to classes. (But I'm getting ahead of myself.)

Writing was always highly emphasized at our school, and as part of our planning for instruction and testing, we were provided "released items" from CSAP so we could analyze what strong responses looked like and share them with our students.[10]

---

[9] More math question samples can be found at www.schoolmattersfoundation.org/testing
[10] https://www.cde.state.co.us/assessment/coassess-released

I remember the persuasive writing prompt below quite well. It appeared on CSAP in 2010 and was released in 2013:

> Imagine that your family is moving to a new place and your family pet will not be allowed to live there. Write a well-developed letter to persuade the person in authority to allow your pet to live there.

Students were directed to write their response in their test booklet, which dedicated a planning page and then about four lined pages to the activity. I have pulled from the responses available on CDE's webpage to show you examples of each proficiency. I entered each response as it appears on the website, errors and formatting intact. Any names used in the samples have been changed by me for privacy. The comments at the bottom were written by the person evaluating the writing.

The writing below is proficient, as you can see from its rating at the bottom. I would consider it a high 3; it has ample reasoning and includes figurative language ("he's the brother I've never had"). My colleague thought it was a 4. Notice that the state evaluator criticized both the ideas and the sentence structure.

Dear Person in authority,

    I have a pet turtle. My parents said that he can't come to my new house. A turtle should be allowed! He dosen't smell and he dosen't make any noise! His tank only needs to be cleaned twice a year. He is cool, can swim very well, is very smart, and he can't bite you. This is not just my pet, or my friend, he's the brother I've never had. Please let him stay.

Sincerely,
Mark

Comments: This response is focused but the topic is not fully developed. The student provides many reasons why the pet should be allowed but does not elaborate on any of the reasons stated. There is a logical progression of ideas. The essay contains age-appropriate words and mostly simple sentence structures. Errors do not impede meaning.

Rating: 3

The response below is partially proficient, as you can see from its rating of 2. I could see why; remember that this is a sixth-grade writer. He has not stated his main idea (restating the prompt), and his sentence structure should be beyond simple at this stage. He should also understand that he needs embedded details to develop his topic. This response looks like the author spent about five minutes, tops, coming up with a cute response to a writing prompt.

Dear Authority,

I know we are not allowed to have cats and dogs at this place. My dog is very well trained and could hand himself very nicely. He can also fold napkins and do many other things too. You should just give him a chance to live there.

sincerely,

The new person

Comments: Relevant information is provided by supporting details are lacking. When the student states "folding napkins" the reader needs to infer what the writer is trying to convey. The fluency of the paper is choppy. There is a logical progression of ideas. The essay contains common words and simple sentences.

Rating: 2

The rating of 1 on the next response seems appropriate. This is a sixth grader, after all. While he does have a reason for his opinion, it is nearly impossible to tell what the writing prompt was from simply reading this response. The errors are also significant enough to inhibit comprehension. (Remember that a rating of 1 means the writer exhibits skills at least two levels below grade level expectations.)

My cat's are well behave. They Don't go in the House Because their well trained. so pleas let us let a cat's live with us.

Comments: This paper only contains one reason why the cat should be allowed to live there (well-trained). The essay is missing [an] introduction and only has a brief concluding sentence. Simple words and sentence structures are used. There are numerous errors in this short piece.

Rating: 1

And finally, here is an advanced response:

> Governor of Denver,
>   This weekend my family and I are moving to your town. I have a dog named Buddy that I've had my whole life. I do not understand why you have denied his living there. He will not cause trouble for he will be in a fenced yard. He is not in prime so he will not breed. Buddy is an old dog that has never harmed anything. So, out of the goodness of your heart, please accept my dear old friend into Denver.
>   Sincerely,
>   Andy L.
>
>
> **Comments:** This response is focused and clearly develops the topic. The supporting details are relevant and specific (in a fenced yard, will not breed and has never harmed anyone) . The paper has a beginning, middle and end. The words are accurate, and a variety of sentence structures are used.
>
> Rating: 4

It is likely our sixth-grade team would have agreed with the advanced rating it received. Not only does it contain complex sentences, it has a quality we call *voice*, which means the writer has shown investment in the writing and has used vocabulary carefully. The word choices seem designed to elicit a certain emotional response, a technique that advanced writers share. There is also a satisfying concluding sentence that contains a high degree of persuasion.

Note that all four of these responses were written by hand in test booklets. I doubt that a child who does not know how to touch type would persist in typing any of these responses in text boxes as they appear here, particularly the two that were marked proficient or above.

Teaching to the test. Do we really do that?

At one time, many years ago, I never would have believed we would teach only what we knew was being tested. That makes very little sense, since all learning is cumulative. But with the stakes as high as they were getting, it seems unavoidable that what we taught *would* gradually shift to what was being tested at our grade level. In sixth grade, for example, we noticed around 2012 that students had been required to write a persuasive essay on CSAP for several years in a row. Not a story. Not a personal narrative. Not an informational piece. A persuasive essay. So we focused on persuasion. We researched every possible way we could instill proficiency and provided numerous essays and paragraphs on which to practice. I presumed that other grade levels did the same with their own CSAP mode of writing.

The thing about education, though, is that it is *supposed to be cumulative.* Each skill is introduced at a fairly young age. Ideally, our students had been writing age-appropriate persuasive opening statements since first and second grades, something along the lines of "I like basketball better than baseball." The early strategies for getting children to be able to write persuasively involve helping them form opinions about topics and share those opinions in writing. That opening statement penned by a second grader might have been followed by a third-grade paragraph something like this:

I like basketball better than baseball. Basketball uses a net. I like throwing things high. My brother plays basketball in high school. Finally, basketball is cool because Lebron James plays it.

In fourth grade, the student would evolve to not only sharing his opinion, but trying to persuade his audience to adopt the same opinion:

Basketball is a better sport than baseball or football. You can play it anywhere. You can play it any time because it is played inside. You can play it even if you don't have enough people. Basketball is throwing large balls into hoops with nets. It is more fun than trying to throw a weird-shaped ball or hit a really small ball. These are my reasons for loving basketball. Don't you think you like it best now, too?

By the time that student reaches sixth grade, he should be able to write a persuasive paragraph that contains multiple reasons as well as embedded details about those reasons. His sentence structure should also be more advanced than the samples you see above.

A proficient sixth grade persuasive paragraph about basketball might look like this:

Basketball is a great sport, don't you think? For one thing, the beginning skills to play it are pretty easy to learn. Once you've done that, you can focus on developing those skills to even better levels. Another great thing about basketball is that you can play it almost anywhere: inside or outside, at a park or on someone's driveway. All you need is a net and at least one person to play it with. This is why basketball is better than baseball, which always needs a lot of people to get a game going.

Teaching writing in sixth grade was always enjoyable, because the lower grade levels in our school did a very good job at instilling the prerequisite skills needed for a student to be able to write like this when he reached sixth grade.

Around 2015, however, I noticed that many of my incoming sixth graders did not know how to write the opinion sentence they should have learned in second grade. They also did not know how to think of reasons for their opinion. I kept seeing sentence fragments like, "Because it's fun." In addition, they were at a loss about the persuasive part of getting the reader to adopt their opinion. They should have been working on this in fourth and fifth grades: I shouldn't have had to start at first base.

And then it occurred to me: those concepts were no longer being taught at the younger grade levels. Everyone was focusing on their own grade level's test writing mode to the exclusion of any other mode. Fifth graders, for instance, had been writing an informational essay on CSAP for several years. All their instruction was probably aimed in that direction.

So much for not teaching to the test!

I noticed that all joking about that, something we had done a lot in the early years of CSAP, had stopped. I guess it had become more uncomfortable than funny to jest about something that had most likely evolved to be true.

Accommodations and Modifications

An equally unsavory shift in our testing protocols was the concept of accommodation for students we thought might not test well otherwise.

Pre-2012, that idea applied to those students with recognized and documented special needs, such as those with medical issues or cognitive difficulties (think: special ed.)

Accommodations were implemented in a classroom based on the student's IEP, a legal document. [11] The purpose was so these special needs students could receive tools or strategies that made learning easier for them. The Edu-speak for this is "more accessible". For instance, a teacher might ask her aide to read the social studies lesson with a student orally in the hall so he can comprehend the material before doing his assignment. Accommodations for children with learning disorders (who have an IEP) are mandated by the ADA. [12]

When differentiation became the mandate in our school, accommodations and modifications were included in the mix.

"It's what's best for kids," we were told.

And we, of course, supported that. These two concepts are supposed to level the playing field for students who have difficulty learning. They were touted as a Best Practice for our struggling students. Our supervisors expected to see them in action during any observation. We did our best to comply, collaborating with the special ed teacher.

What's the difference between accommodations and modifications? It has to do with the learning *environment* verses the learning *material.*

> "Accommodation refers to the change in the procedures applied or used in a certain area to attend to a task. However, **what is being measured by the task or challenge is not changed** in this case. In a classroom situation, for example, a student may be given additional time to finish an assessment test for them to minimize distractions. In such a case, **the procedures of the test** will be modified or 'accommodated' to help the student to succeed. However, the way the test will be graded or how the student will be assessed after the test will not be changed.

---

[11] IEP: Individualized Education Program
[12] ADA: Americans with Disabilities Act, 1990.

Other Examples of Accommodation:
- Hands-on activities
- Seating in front of a room for average or poorly performing students.
- Allowing students to take a test in quieter environments.
- Additional tutoring time.
- Working in smaller groups
- Giving a student study guides from the teachers.
- Reducing the homework or assignment workload.
- Establishing extra communication between the teacher, student, and involving their parents.
- Applying positive reinforcement behavior strategies.
- Getting sign language interpreters for students with hearing complications.
- Offering large-print learning materials."

Modifications, on the other hand, deal with the material, itself, as seen here:

"Modification refers to a situation where **what is being assessed or measured is changed,** but the procedures are not modified. In a classroom setup, for example, a student may be given an oral spelling test instead of a written one. In this case, the actual test or assessment will have been changed, but the procedure of doing it will remain the same.

Other Examples of Modification:
- Allowing a student to use a calculator during an exam assessment.
- Reducing the number of similar questions in a test.
- Reducing reading levels.
- Simplifying the lessons that a student takes to increase their level of understanding.
- Simplifying the vocabulary used.
- Adjusting the grading level, for instance, to weighted grading." [13]

These measures might be used to assist someone reading at a third-grade level to understand and assimilate the concepts presented in a sixth-grade science book. That was the purpose, usually: to make learning the grade level material in a subject area accessible for students with reading difficulties.

Then things changed dramatically.

---

[13] Brown, Sarah. "Difference Between Accommodations and Modifications." 2019.

In the fall of 2012, we were maneuvered into designating accommodations to any student we suspected might not do well on TCAP. [14]

We were told to monitor our students closely and determine which might benefit from accommodations. **If accommodations were implemented and documented by October 1, they could be used on the state's test in March.**

Here are some of the things it was suggested we look for:

- Needing extra time on written work
- Needing a scribe (someone to write what a child dictates)
- Needing directions read aloud

Imagine the implications of this. Because a teacher began documenting in late September that Suzie needs things written for her, Suzie is able to test privately with an aide who will write everything for her. There is no evidence required to back up the teacher's documentation. We were encouraged to use this accommodation for students with extremely poor handwriting or who had a habit of not developing a topic fully.

A teacher could also document that Peter needs the directions read aloud to him even though he has no reading comprehension deficits. His biggest challenge is staying focused and actually *noticing* directions before plunging into an assignment, so the teacher figures if he has someone making sure he pays attention to directions (and therefore, controlling how quickly he moves through the test), he will do better on it.

We were told by Gary Morris that, **by law**, if the accommodation was documented at least three times, even if just written in a planning book, it could be implemented during TCAP.

It seemed clear that the only purpose for including accommodations for non-IEP students was to inflate our school's scores. The nefariousness of this bothered me immensely.

It was implicitly understood by all of us that for this management of scores to fly under the radar, we couldn't go overboard in our documentations of supposedly necessary accommodations. Still, our school had so many of

---

[14] TCAP: Transitional Colorado Assessment Program - The successor to CSAP in Colorado, a very similar test

them that when testing time came, every aide from every corner was re-assigned to administer testing to those students with accommodations.

It also became clear to me that everyone, from state officials down to school principals, wanted test scores to be inflated. Otherwise, why tell us we could do it?

This is perhaps the most insidious of the changes we underwent beginning in 2012. And we ate it up because it was couched in pleasant language:

"best for kids"
"research-based"
"good for our school"
"level the playing field"

I was a rare standout. I would not document accommodations that were not necessary. To me, it seemed like fraud.

Maneuvering Test Outcomes

During testing time, teachers become proctors, people who administer a test. We have yearly training for this: new policies are shared and old policies that don't pass the smell test are outlawed.

In my former district, we were told we could make sweeping comments to an entire room, such as "Make sure you read everything carefully." We could not make that comment to an individual student. We were instructed to look over the shoulders of our students to check their work (surreptitiously) and if we saw an issue, we should think of something to announce to the whole room, while looking at that child.

Another technique in our school was to outlaw 'early finishing'. Students were not allowed to close their booklets during the 60-minute session. This was when testing was still done in large paper booklets, prior to 2016. Students could not indicate in any manner that they were finished, either by closing the booklet, putting their head down, or reading a novel at their desk.

Instead, the teacher would quietly advise the student to go through the test again and look at each test item carefully. (Why this private comment was allowed, I don't know.) Additionally, we were told to examine our students' handwriting and instruct them to write neater or erase parts and re-do them to improve the legibility.

An even more alarming aspect of test manipulation, however, is what we did after the students finished testing. From 2005 through 2014, we teachers were required to look through our test booklets, erasing stray marks that might cause erroneous scoring and darkening the pencil marks in the answers chosen. We did this as a group, ostensibly to ensure that no one was changing a student's answers.

The reality is that it was entirely possible to change an answer, because everyone was concentrating on her own stack of books. If one of my colleagues did something other than erase stray marks or darken existing ones, I wouldn't have known, because I was busy with my own stack, and because I couldn't see their book from their vantage point. The likelihood is that even if I suspected cheating, I wouldn't have mentioned it, as it is extremely uncomfortable to accuse a peer of wrongdoing.

When this practice suddenly ended in 2015, I surmised that the district had gotten wind of it. The orientation language that year specifically banned teachers from touching student booklets other than to distribute them and collect them. They began to be stored under lock and key in an empty room that only our test coordinator – Gary Morris – could access.

State testing went entirely digital the next year, and I assumed that security was part of the reason. Without human hands touching test booklets, the process was less prone to human corruption. But what have we sacrificed to accomplish this? Children as young as eight years old are required to explain their thinking by typing in text boxes. How realistic does this seem? When someone uses the hunt-and-peck method of typing, he is less likely to expand upon his ideas. I've seen it in my own classes: children type the minimum or skip that step altogether because it's just not 'fun'.

And because it doesn't matter to *them* whether they get a good score on the test. It's merely another piece of drudgery to be endured.

Best practices in education indicate that children learn best when they have choice, opportunity, challenge, and rigorous expectations.

15 The First Step: Accountability

Almost every teacher agrees with the statement on the opposite page. The point of this book is not that modern approaches to differentiating a child's education are not effective; quite the contrary. Even John Hattie's ideas have some merit. Colorado's legislature also most likely had good intentions rather than teacher hatred in their hearts when they wrote and passed SB 10-191.

Good intentions, however, often pave the road to poor results. Differentiation and other forms of best practices in teaching are laudable, but they are not *doable* within current class sizes. Merit pay may *seem* laudable, but offering it raises the stakes to levels that encourage fraud. Holding teachers accountable *is* laudable, but any evaluation system based on observation is subject to the biases of *humans*. In addition, there is no realistic way to hold teachers accountable without also holding students accountable.

Incredibly, this last one is a tough concept to get some people to understand. The best way might be to help them see it from their perspective as an employee. What if your evaluation as a 911 operator relied on whether those who call in use the 911 system correctly? Or your evaluation as an MD was based on how many of your patients followed your advice?

When we hold teachers accountable for the test performance of their students, we are absolving students of their own responsibility. The onus to prove what he knows should be placed on the student. And that includes the testing we do to determine how to direct a student's differentiated learning, something I mentioned briefly in chapter 5. We call these tests, given at various times across the school year, *'formative assessments'*, and a major testing organization that provides them is NWEA, with their MAP Growth assessment.[1] If you peruse their website, you see that this organization does, indeed, provide a lot of insight about student achievement and readiness through its testing. There are multiple reports a teacher can generate and study to determine just where a student's areas of need are.

The issue I have is the divide between this terrific resource and the buy-in from students taking the assessments. The kids *know* there is nothing riding on the outcome for them. Not only that, there is an even more dismal aspect to this type of data collection: the more we test, the more blasé our students become about it.

It continues to confound me that the education elites don't get this.

Our administrators also put zero stock in student accountability; they truly believe that the onus lies on us, often lecturing us about it: '*Look, you have one job on test day: make your students take the test seriously. If they don't, that's on you.*'

Here's what I noticed when I watched my students take a MAP math test in January 2014. Many of them doodled on their scratch paper. Others stared at monitors without moving the scroll bar, then clicked an answer at the bottom of the screen. Around half of them seemed intent on reading the material fully and sometimes doing the work on their paper prior to clicking an answer.

As I walked around the computer lab, I stopped behind the chairs of students that I felt confident about as well as those I thought would struggle. When I stopped behind Nick's chair, here is what I saw on his screen:

A class of 24 students shares a set of 100 crayons.
If four students are absent, which of these statements is true?

    a.   For every 4 students, there is 1 crayon
    b.   For each student, there are 5 crayons.
    c.   For each student, there are 4 crayons
    d.   For every 5 students, there is 1 crayon

Nick looked up at me. "What do you think?" he mouthed.

"I think you should choose your answer," I had said quietly.

He started counting off on his fingers, eventually stopping at his ring finger. He then clicked answer *C* and grinned up at me.

"What was that?" I asked suspiciously.

"Eenie Meenie Minie Moe," he said. "Works every time."

---

[1] NWEA: Northwest Evaluation Association, www.nwea.org/. MAP: Measures of Academic Progress.

"Why are you doing that?" I asked him. "You *know* this. You're in advanced math!"

"It's more fun this way," he had said.

You might remember from early in this book that I mentioned Nick as a very bright kid whom I was warned had no filter and liked to rankle Monica. His outspokenness did not bother me because I knew there was a purpose to it. He always brought something thought-provoking to the table. While I was disappointed in his attitude toward the test, I couldn't blame him. The sad thing, though, is how jaded he was by age 12. But that often happens with our brightest minds. They know the education system is not set up for them and, usually, they just deal with it.

Sometimes, they have fun with it.

As I moved on, I came to Nikki. She was new to our school and had latched onto Monica in a hero worship kind of way. She was not nearly as bright or motivated as Monica, however, and chose to mostly draw balloons in class.

Nikki clicked her *'next'* button and a new question popped up. I saw her head bob as she appeared to be reading the question. Then she studied her fingernails, biting on one of them, drew a balloon on her scratch paper, and filled it with mini balloons. Eventually she selected answer *C*. Looking at the log of previous questions she had answered, I saw a pattern of *C, D, A, B, C*.

Don't tell me; let me guess: the next answer is D. I was not wrong.

I watched her click to the next question, give a short period of time waiting, and then type in *A*.

Not everyone chose answers according to their own inner pattern. I did see students with heads bent over scratch paper, apparently deep in thought. But not many. Our policy was to collect the scratch paper afterward and dispose of it. As I glanced through the sheets, I saw a lot of doodling.

How do you **make** someone test seriously? Even if they look like they're serious, how can you know they're not just staring and then clicking after a decent amount of time has passed?

MAP does have a teacher alert that lets you know from your own monitor if a child is clicking an answer too soon after the question has been posed. Don't tell me the Nicks of the world haven't figured that little trick out after a few times of my saying quietly, "Make sure you read the question thoroughly."

I'm reluctant to say, 'Don't test the children', but test scores only work for gathering data if the learners are invested. Are our children invested?

Let's think about this from a child's point of view. He's in sixth grade, about 12 years old, reading a paragraph that poses some scenario in which he will have to perform, say, four mathematical functions before he can come to the final, correct, answer. He must type his preliminary steps in separate boxes to show his thought process. There are hidden processes he must discover to get to the correct endpoint. Furthermore, he cannot bounce ideas off anyone, as he has been doing all year in *non*-test situations. (This is what best practices in learning assures us will make the learning stick.)

Now imagine there are twenty problems just like this, each one an exhaustive procedure. How many adults do you know who would tackle an assessment like this earnestly, without some assurance there would be advancement in his career or pay? No one I know would do that.

In 2020, I took a test on Reading Instruction Theory as part of getting my New Mexico teaching license. There were 150 theory and hypothetical situation questions, with a time limit of 180 minutes. It was the hardest test I've taken, ever. I was near tears at one point when I realized I didn't know what *prosody* means, gleaning from the questions that it must be a critical part of reading comprehension. I used every ounce of inference ability I possessed to find out what it could mean as I read each subsequent question. I then went back to the questions I had earmarked and changed my answers according to what I realistically thought '*prosody*' means. Do you think I would have put that much effort into an assessment that had no bearing on my career? I assure you, I would not. [2]

Yet, this is exactly the test behavior we expect of our students when they are taking standardized tests. We coach them with practice tests; we give them pep talks: we teach the skills tactics I described above. How much success do you think we have when the child finally sits down and begins looking at questions that require a great deal of thought, inference, and re-working?

I passed that test with 85% accuracy and was rewarded with a seven-year teaching license and a huge sense of relief. I doubt I would have endured that test and tried as hard as I did just because someone at the state level told me they needed accurate data on how well teachers understand reading instruction theory.

If we're going to test students, let's be realistic about what they *should* know and when. *And* how real life handles problem-solving. And then, let's

---

[2] *Prosody* means reading text with expression, whether orally or in one's head, a technique that improves comprehension. I had taught this to my students for decades without knowing the term for what I was doing!

hold the kids accountable for their performance. It's time we stop kidding ourselves: the only way to get an accurate measure of what anyone *can* do is provide incentive to give their best.

And finally...
Standardized testing and the practice of awarding accommodations to any child we want exist in contradiction to one another. If the intent of Common Core was to make learning a more rigorous enterprise, why is it necessary to manipulate the scores reported on tests that are created to co-exist with Common Core?

When I arrived home that afternoon, I found my daughter Cassidy cooking dinner.[3] It was a pleasant surprise because she wasn't often home when I got there.

She noticed that I was preoccupied and asked me about it. I shared how unseriously my students had taken their MAP tests that week, especially math. She grinned at me, and when I stopped focusing on my own angst for a moment, it occurred to me to wonder why.

I was then informed that even my own child had not always tested seriously during CSAP.

"Do you remember how bad my scores in sophomore year were?" she asked me.

I did but reminded her that she had been sick at the time.

She shook her head. "No. That's just what I told you when you got the results."

I had stared at her. "What do you mean?"

"I randomly pressed answers without reading them," she told me.

I was stunned.

"My friends and I had a bet. We wanted to see if our scores would follow the random guessing bell curve if we took the test without reading anything but the questions. We all swore we would do it."

---

[3] Not her real name, but this conversation with my daughter did happen as I have described it. I used it to inspire a conversation between Wendy Taylor and her daughter in *Finishing School*, the companion novel to this book.

I was at a loss for words. That CSAP test hadn't had any bearing on her life, in any way whatsoever. The scores didn't follow her anywhere, the way SAT or ACT scores do. From her point of view, it was a good choice for an experiment on random guessing. And a complete waste of time. I couldn't say she was wrong.

Later that week, I was enjoying a science lesson with my students when Gary Morris peeked into my room, clipboard in hand. We were taking notes on the properties of matter after a very rousing activity in which students pretended to be molecules. An important concept for junior learners regarding matter is that the molecules are always moving to some degree. Even in solids, the molecules vibrate. The kids who are chosen to be solid molecules always have fun vibrating in their 'molecular group', but those who are gases have even more fun floating all over the room.

"Okay, everyone," I said as smoothly as possible, "put your spiral in the air to show me how far you are on your notes. Everyone should have the T-chart drawn with the headings *Physical Properties* and *Chemical Properties*." Using my laser pointer, I focused their attention to the front whiteboard. I looked around the room at the raised spirals and continued. "Remember that I will look at your notes during lunch time. Make sure they are ready for inspection."

I saw Morris writing on his clipboard.

"Now," I continued, "stop what you are doing. With your partner, discuss the idea of physical and chemical properties and how you might use them if you were, say, the first inventor of cars."

I walked around the room, listening to conversations, while Morris continued scribbling.

"How can you be the first inventor of something, Ms. Zempel?" Nick asked when I reached him.

"What?" I said absently, glancing sideways in Morris' direction.

"If you're the inventor," Nick continued, "you *are* the first." He laughed at his cleverness. Then he beckoned me to put my ear down to his mouth. Curious, I complied. "Are we doing this because Mr. Morris is watching?" he whispered.

I grinned at him and whispered back, "Of course. Thanks for playing along."

Nick winked. "I think it's funny how you adults are always so serious about everything," he whisper-mouthed to me.

I smiled at him. "So do I, Nick."

'Teacher training' usually does nothing but check off
government-required boxes on forms for teachers,
and make the people giving the training that much richer.
It also gives the administration and politicians
some cover for problems.

"We'll fix this problem via better training" is a good way
to get complainers off your back for a while,
until, hopefully, they forget about the complaint. [4]

---

[4] Bates, Matthew. "What must schools prioritize to better address the needs of students..." 2022.

16 Professional Development

Stacking the Deck

In school year 2017-18, our professional development sessions involved one of our third-grade colleagues regaling us every few weeks with how well best practices were working in her classroom. (She was one of the ten who had flown to Chicago the previous summer.)

She would arrive with visuals and student work samples and PowerPoint presentations of how she was employing the strategies successfully in her room. I would stare in awe as she described all her third graders productively employed in their different tasks while she worked with small groups at her reading table. I assumed that either she was very good at teaching and classroom management, or her classroom had been stacked with particularly earnest students. That latter assumption was really more of a snarky jealous thought. I couldn't believe that any principal would deviate from the time-honored practice of loading all classrooms equally with our student roster. Watching her presentations, I usually waffled between inspiration at how she was able to make everything work and wondering if there were *any* moments at all when it didn't.

Then, during one break from a day-long teacher in-service, I chatted with one of my former sixth grade colleagues who had moved to third grade. I mentioned how amazing it was that Ms. Wonderful's techniques were so successful, while I struggled almost every day.

> *"I guess it's just the difference between third grade and sixth grade," I had mused.*
>
> *My colleague smiled at me, shaking her head. "She has an edge."*

"What's that?" I asked.

"She has an aide with her all day."

"How is that possible?" I asked in disbelief.

My colleague shrugged. "She also has the best students in third grade. No special ed. No ELL's[1] *No kids with a known behavior history. And only 22 students."*

I stared in disbelief.

"Oh, believe me," she said. "I've counted."

No one in our school had a full-time aide. The closest anyone came was kindergarten. It was not possible, according to the budget, our principal always said. Each grade level of four or five teachers was given around 15 hours of aide time *per week* to divide up among their teachers. I had an aide for an hour and a half at most 3 times a week.

We worked with kids in our classrooms for more than six hours a day. It was unthinkable that one cherry-picked teacher who also happened to be lecturing us on how well differentiation and other best practices work in a classroom had another adult in her room for that entire time helping to make it happen. Not only did she have *an* aide, she had one of the very *best* aides, one who had worked in our school for many years and was sought-after by most other teachers in the primary grades.

It is this type of situation that creates unrest and cynicism. Our principal apparently had an agenda, possibly one that would further his own career, and had created a utopian classroom to prove his theories. After every presentation this colleague made, our principal wasted no time lecturing us that we, too, could have her kind of success, if only we would use the strategies she used. I wondered how many district bigwigs had been brought over to view that classroom and marvel at how our principal had been able to achieve so much with limited resources.

I also wondered how this information had not escaped through the grapevine, but in a school our size (more than 1,100 students), I supposed it was possible, particularly if our principal had moles in different grade levels, cozying up at every opportunity. (Additionally, every teacher comes to know unequivocally that the adage "go along to get along" applies doubly in a school.)

It's safe to say that after that conversation, I no longer listened to these lectures with the same interest. But I did still take notes.

---

[1] ELL = English Language Learner

What Are 'Best Practices'...Really?

That term has become a common buzz phrase in education, and it is often used to either manipulate teachers or convince them that you know what you're talking about. So let's get back to basics and find out what it originally meant.

After a very quick internet search using this question:
What does 'best practices' mean for a teacher?
... I found this answer:

Best Practices in education:
The teaching strategies teachers use daily began as innovative ideas that were tested and then perfected by their creators. This suggests that the definition for best practices can be interpreted as **existing teaching practices that have been proven to be effective**. [2]

The online site where I found this definition also features an article that delineates five best practices that I would say get to the heart of what quality teaching looks like: [3]

1. Plan, plan, plan
Teaching and planning are inseparable friends, and for good reason. With a solid plan in place, you'll be able to teach your class more smoothly. Planning also allows for logical progression in teaching and learning, backup activities for unpredictable events, and fewer chances for behavioral issues to pop up among students.

2. Endgame goals
Goals are another driving force in teaching. Both teachers and students alike should have clear goals in the classroom. As teachers, we have learning and behavioral goals for students and, hopefully, some aspirational goals for ourselves, too — after all, we can always improve our own teaching, even if we're seasoned veterans. Students need to be taught how to set goals for themselves and how to work toward achieving them.

3. Communication is key
Communication — you know, that thing we do all the time — cannot be overlooked when it comes to teaching best practices. It's important in any

---

[2] Classful.com/best-practices-in-education
[3] Melissa Williams. "What are the Best Practices in Teaching?" 2019

relationship, and you most definitely (hopefully?) have a relationship with your students and their families. The need for good communication also extends to interactions with your colleagues — establishing and maintaining communication with your teacher pals will allow for collaboration, fresh ideas, and a little help here and there!

4. Model teacher = model students

The next cornerstone of A+ teaching practices is modeling behavior. Talk the talk and walk the walk consistently, and your students will be far more likely to follow suit.

Some areas to focus on when modeling behavior include showing respect for others, reading more often, and being a good audience member and listener. If students see you being respectful to them and to your colleagues, they will understand the value that you put on respect and will see firsthand what respect looks like in practice. Good manners are contagious, so spread them around!

5. Check for Understanding

Last — but certainly not least — is the art of checking for understanding. How should you go about doing this? There are about as many options available for checking understanding as there is variety in the types of learners in your classroom.

There are the classic regular standbys that check for understanding, such as tests and quizzes, but you should always be sprinkling in alternative methods for checking knowledge. For example, consider working in some observation times (particularly during group work) so you can walk around the classroom and check in on everyone's progress. You could also have your students do oral presentations and assessments, reflections, summaries, and think-pair-shares, to name a few.

Combine this very simple list of teacher practices with quality teaching materials, and you have 2/3 of a smart recipe for success. So why is it any more complicated than that?

My theory: it's because **education has been hijacked by people who have infused it with grandiose jargon designed to make teaching (and learning) seem too sophisticated for most of us to understand.** If you doubt this, go back to page 137 and peruse some of the web pages I cited.

Every administrator is heavily influenced by what you see on the CDE's website; that fact lends itself to how schools are managed and how teachers are trained. It's a disquieting thought, but discussion of educational practices, using scholarly terms, has become more valuable than the practices themselves. Everyone in education is rewarded for this: teachers and principals looking to further their careers, school board members wishing for a better political landscape, and even researchers hoping for the next Big Idea. Scholarly discussion has been the mainstay of professional development for *years*, and its offshoot, the scholarly *documentation* that teachers create, has proliferated the farce.

Why must teachers document? Because that documentation will compel their principal to give them a high rating on those indicators of teaching performance [4] and in turn, allow that principal to check boxes on her *own* paperwork for the district, which then submits *its* documentation to the state. *It's a circular system built on compliance, which must, according to the powers that be, remain intact.* (In fact, even the professional development *sessions* are documented as part of the paperwork administrators submit to their district.)

Why would the people in charge support such a façade? It seems counterintuitive if our goal is to help children learn. But maybe that's not the goal. Maybe the goal has more to do with keeping the machine operational.

Someone, somewhere, should be able to connect the dots here: all this....scholarly activity has not made a difference in student achievement in Colorado, or even nationwide.

It's time to return education to its original aims: teaching children to read, write, and cipher. It's really very simple to do these things, *if* you have the time to sit with a child and train him in phonics, grammar, syntax, and number sense.

Let's revisit the words of Dr. James Delisle, from page 16:

Differentiation in practice is harder to implement in a heterogeneous classroom than it is to juggle with one arm tied behind your back.

Differentiation *must* be the goal in effective education. Once teachers understand that and we enable its implementation, professional development can take on a very different (and much more useful) path: what individual teaching teams see as *their* need. [5]

The resources to enhance instruction and enable learning are nearly endless. You can find almost anything you need, whether on the internet or in books. On the next few pages, I'll discuss three of the more than 25 books from my own collection and how they impacted my teaching. Then I'll share why *any* strategies currently miss the mark.

---

[4] See page 122 or Appendix A on page 216.
[5] See points 1 and 2 in chapter 18.

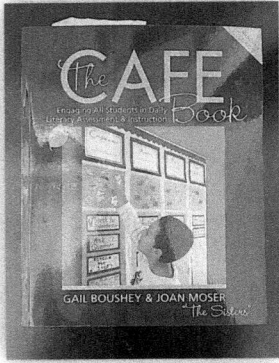

The CAFÉ Book, developed by a pair of teaching sisters, is a program that structures literacy around a daily schedule and promotes student choice. We were encouraged to use this program in 2014, which I did for a year. What I found was that there was too much unsupervised activity in the room and students appeared to be pretending to participate, but their "choice" activity had more to do with messing around than learning. I do, however, believe that with fewer students and more adults in a classroom, this approach can be successful.

The CAFÉ system incorporates what the authors call "The Daily Five" into a child's school day:

- Read to Yourself
- Read to Someone Else
- Work on Writing
- Listen to Reading
- Work on words (vocabulary study)

Children are tasked to move themselves through the rotation of activities. Remember when I wrote about motivation? A great deal of it is required when you have independent activities like this and children *moving freely around a classroom*, switching activities when *they* are ready, not at a signal given by the teacher. Excellent strategy but it needs purposeful monitoring. Keep it in mind when you read my proposals for classroom revision in the chapter 18.

Reading Nonfiction is one of the best manuals I've studied about how to make nonfiction useful to students. In my experience, many intermediate students do not care for reading novels, especially the boys. And that should be okay. It's nonfiction comprehension, really, that will determine their academic success in high school and college.

Rather than shaming students for not enjoying fiction, I encouraged them to study subjects they were interested in and then find books and internet articles on

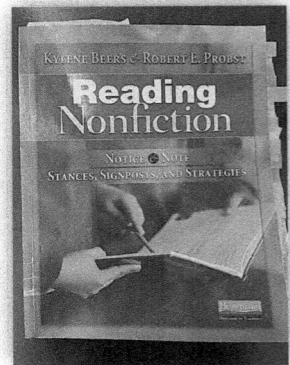

those topics. Occasionally, that interest in sports would lead them to a novel centered around baseball or another sport.

Making Thinking Visible was inspired by a five-year Harvard University study on how child learning can be effectively implemented. I studied this book as part of my GT graduate program; it is so packed with substance that it could comprise a semester-long class on its own.

Here are some of the notable tenets described in the book:

- Have students make Maps of Understanding for what they study.
- Model authentic questioning rather than obviously contrived questioning. (Kids can see through that.)
- Establish thinking routines. They provide a structure that kids can rely on, and if there is a structure, students are more likely to place value on it.
- Make room for reflection. Reflection is a way to promote metacognitive thinking, which many experts recognized as an effective way to make learning 'stick'.
- Promote classroom discussion and teach appropriate protocols for respectful discussion.

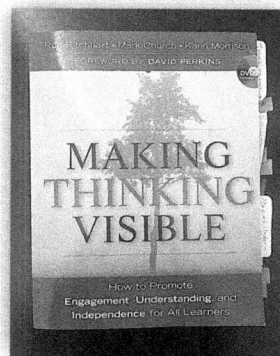

One type of discussion activity is the Micro Lab, explained here:

The Micro Lab Protocol

Reflect individually on the issue or topic being examined; then, working in triads:
- Share: The first person in the group shares for a set time (usually 1-2 minutes). The other members listen without comment or interruption.
- Pause for 20-30 seconds of silence to take in what was said.
- Repeat for persons two and three, pausing for a moment of silence after each round.
- Discuss as a group (5-10 minutes), referencing the comments that have been made and making connections between the responses of the group.

The rationale for developing this type of approach is explained by the authors like this:

> Teachers often ask groups to discuss ideas in classrooms with more and less success. Often groups get sidetracked and/or a single person dominates while others sit back. Micro Lab is designed to ensure equal participation and make sure everyone contributes...This keeps all groups on track and focused. [6]

Does it? Take a class of 30 fifth, seventh, or twelfth graders. Dividing them into "triads" means you will have ten groups of discussion going on simultaneously. Even if kids are talking in whisper voices (not likely), the din from so much activity could be extremely counterproductive. I have tried the Micro Lab in my sixth-grade classes, even demonstrating the techniques with one group of three while the rest observed. Even with this training, it was not a successful enterprise. There is little incentive to comply with the rules for the Micro Lab, and there is only one teacher walking around the classroom listening to discussions and asking probing questions of the learners. How can she be sure all her students are fully focused on the topic?

The Micro Lab sounds like it could be an effective small group discussion strategy. Let's try it with much smaller classes, though, and more than one adult supervising and guiding the groups.

I have found useful information from every book I've studied; there is little issue regarding the programs and strategies proposed by well-intended and knowledgeable persons over the last several decades.

My concern has to do with implementation, and it is two-fold:

First, the disconnect between these ideas and their practical use in classrooms where the students are not invested.

Second, the elephant in the room that is ignored by nearly everyone: teachers are asked to do more and more for each pupil under their charge, without considering whether it is even possible.

Proposing strategies without addressing the issues that stand in their way promotes havoc, and in turn, chaos, because no teacher can ever be fully successful, but everyone feels the squeeze of the expectation that they *can* be, if only they try harder.

---

[6] Ritchhart, Church, and Morrison. *Making Thinking Visible: How to Promote Engagement, Understanding, and Independence for All Learners.* 2011, p. 147

It is our character that supports the promise of our future – far more than particular government programs or policies.

There is no end to the good you can do if you don't care who gets credit for it.[7]

\- William J. Bennett,
former Secretary of Education

---

[7] William J. Bennett, author of *The Book of Virtues*, 1993 by Simon & Schuster; and former Secretary of Education (1985-1988). Quotes accessed from Quote Fancy: https://quotefancy.com/william-j-bennett-quotes

17 The Real Bottom Line

There's an underlying element in education that is unnoticed by most people. Schools are not set up for the children; they are set up for the convenience of the adults who run them. If children were the top priority in a school, they would not be assigned to static class groupings without the opportunity to advance to a different group when *they* are ready.

If children were the top priority, the people who work with them would be seen as more important than the bureaucrats who direct those people. Class groups would not be divided into "fair" sets of upper, middle, and low aptitudes. The behavior problems would not be ignored or rationalized so that every other child has his education seriously diminished by the outlandishness of a few.

If children were truly the reason schools exist, the ratio of adult to child would be a reasonable and realistic one.

Our schools, particularly at the elementary level, are operated with the guiding principles that...

1) Procedures and policies, dutifully followed, meet the education needs of students,
   and
2) Children should be arranged in groupings that are acceptable to the adults in charge.

This is nonsense, but at present, there is little that can be done to thwart these firmly established ideals because the teachers' unions won't allow for a sensible approach to education.

And because of the union strangle-hold on education, a third principle also now exists:

3) Those who work with children must be regulated, lectured, and gaslighted by those who don't.

Politicians and administrators had been stymied for years in their quest to get around the teachers' unions, who set and control how teachers and students are assigned within schools. Perhaps they thought their legislation would mitigate this. But instead of making the situation better, they have made it worse. This is what happens when you try to put a Band-Aid on a cannonball wound. [1]

The story of my career derailment is important to understand because it underscores how corrupt-prone teacher evaluation systems are, regardless of how couched in polite terms they may be.

Re-read the indicators of teaching success on page 122. Do *you* think it is possible for a principal who visits a teacher's room perhaps three times per year to absolutely *know* how to rate her on any of them? He would have to be in the classroom almost constantly *and* be witness to every non-teaching activity she does, such as communicating with parents or planning what resources to bring into the classroom.

Additionally, a principal could go either way on almost every indicator, depending on how much he does or doesn't want the teacher to get a high mark. The list of standards is designed to appease people in power. It is not designed to ensure learning for children.

This type of teacher evaluation creates undue stress on every teacher in the building, even those who are in favor, who operate with both the uncertainty that their favored status will last *and* the guilt of being in that favored class in the first place.

Prior to 2012, when evaluation systems had no real backbone; most of us played the game without argument. The stakes for us were nearly nonexistent. But we should have known that a façade such as that could not last. There were too many cases of poor teachers taking advantage of a profession that had become ripe for exploitation by people who wished for an unmonitored career that provided a pension at its conclusion.

In my school, the one where I served for 20 years, we were sheltered from this reality because we were known as a no-nonsense school. Those who wished to coast usually avoided us like the plague.

The real bottom line in education is that teachers should be able to do their job without the distraction of documenting that they *are* doing their job. They should be able to work with children in job assignments that are suited

---

[1] Apologies to Brian Regan, whose comedy special *I Walked on the Moon* inspired my slightly different take on what he actually said.

to their strengths. (They should be counseled to understand that there are many student needs in a school, and personnel will be assigned to meet those needs, not the other way around.)

The current problems in education are shared and exacerbated by everyone involved. The Edu-speak that guides every educator's career, whether teacher or administrator, has become the most important aspect of the game. If one can manipulate these phrases effectively, one will achieve career success. But is this what education is supposed to accomplish?

At the start of school year 2012, when we teachers were coached on using Common Core and Visible Learning ideals for instruction and required to meet for curriculum-parsing and poster-making, I was a vocal detractor. Things didn't make sense, and I shared that in our trainings, believing they were still the collegial environment they had been prior to 2012. I soon learned that we were all now living in a different world, perhaps not of Rebecca's choosing, but she certainly wasn't entirely blameless.

In addition to the new best practices that were now expected, the new evaluation system defied logic. It was a struggle to understand how *anyone* could believe assigning ratings to teachers could possibly be a valid way to assess their performance on the job. Yet everyone spoke as if the system had honor and integrity. (The folktale "The Emperor's New Clothes" often came to mind.)

Teachers work very hard to curry favor with the administrator who gives them their ratings. Only a naïve person would refuse to consider how human nature works in these situations. Butter someone up and you'll be rewarded ten-fold.

My colleague Mary tried multiple times to get me to do that with Gary Morris in the years after his horrible review. I stubbornly resisted, even to the point of declining to meet with him outside my required pre- and post-observation conversations. During those, I always sat stony-faced, taking notes as necessary but always waiting to be dismissed.

In the fall of 2016, I finally decided to change tactics. My curiosity had won out. *Was* it possible to successfully manipulate Gary Morris?

I decided to find out.

Requesting a private meeting with him soon after school started, I showed him a book I had read over the summer (*Reading Nonfiction*, in fact) and said I looked forward to implementing some great new practices. He looked surprised but pleased. I also told him I looked forward to his analysis of how these practices were going. Very little about my actual teaching changed.

At our next meeting, I told him how much I thought I had missed in not taking the changes more seriously at first. I noticed after that conversation there were fewer visits from him.

After each observation, I emailed him and asked for specific hints about improving my practice. I also asked him for advice on choosing my Individual Educator Goals: *I know you miss being in the classroom. What would **you** pick if you had this opportunity?*

Some might say these tactics are just common-sense and professional, but the point is that nothing changed about my classroom demeanor or strategies. I was still teaching the way I had taught for the previous three years, since Morris first became my evaluator, yet suddenly, I was an improved educator because I was stroking his ego.

I did notice my overall stress level decrease, but *should* this be the case? A teacher's sense of well-being is dependent upon how much she can curry favor with her evaluator? At the end of that year, May 2017, my final eval had several *highly effective* marks on it and not one *partially effective*.

The following year (my final year of teaching in Colorado), I decided to up the ante on experimentation. I knew I was going to retire at the end of the year, so I figured I had little to lose. My target this time? The Individual Educator Goals: you know, those student growth goals whose data determined 30% of my evaluation by this time. I gave a baseline and recorded the scores on my grid. Each month thereafter, however, I recorded scores that looked reasonable, based on observations of regular student performance.

At the end of April, I did the same for my final column of scores. No assessment administered. I *did* put thought into it, not wanting to inflate a child's score above what I had observed his ability to be. When I tabulated the "results", my students had 'achieved' 80% growth on the skill, what the district determined was an acceptable measure of learning for an average group of students.[2]

Did this management of supposed outcomes give me a raise for exceptional performance? No, it did not. Did it affect my students in any way? No. It merely met the requirements of a foolish exercise the district had been perpetrating for five years. What we were doing had no value; never, in those five years, had my evaluator asked to see any of the assessments that backed up the data I was reporting. It appeared that no one cared whether

---

[2] I taught math and social studies that year. The skill for this goal was in geography: being able to use an atlas to find random locations in the world. The fact that Gary Morris approved this low-level goal says a lot about how far our professional relationship had progressed. If you'll recall, my first goal in 2013 was a proficient rating on writing an essay!

my students gained anything through this activity; the paperwork to ensure compliance was all that mattered.

If you knew you were in favor, I'm sure it was easy to take this shortcut. The likelihood of being asked for your assessments was low. And even if you *were* asked for them, you could pretend you misplaced the folder or left it at home. (If you were a member of the union, your supervisor *definitely* was not going to press you for the information.)

I found it curious that the subject of growth goals never came up in casual conversation with my colleagues. It seemed that no one wanted to open the can of worms that might entice them to say something they would later regret.

I'm sure the intent of SB 10-191 was to encourage teachers to *want* to reflect on their teaching and to grow from that reflection. I doubt that happens for most teachers, however. In my own school, I saw how easy it could be to turn a district mandate into a shortcut-laden farce. When teachers perceive that a job requirement has no bottom-line value in any regard, they will do whatever they can to adhere to the letter of the law only. The spirt intended by Colorado's General Assembly is not even given a modicum of thought. Even Gary Morris seemed to consider *his* responsibility to supervise goal-setting a waste of time, given how little he appeared to take the process seriously.

Instead of rewarding quality teaching in Colorado, legislators compelled school districts to reward *the appearance of* quality teaching. Getting rid of this phoniness is necessary before our education woes can be fixed. The elites don't want things to change, perhaps because the new normal doesn't affect *them* at all. But for the rest of us, it's excruciating. It is also very easy to forget why we became teachers in the first place.

> Those who are unaffected by onerous requirements
> are more likely to impose those requirements on others.
> This has been the case in school management for decades.

After my retirement from Colorado teaching, I moved to New Mexico to teach a few more years. A recent colleague told me that the general consensus among teachers here is anger. The people in charge do not get it. They don't understand that throwing more money at teachers, with stipulations attached, is not helping them do their job. The bureaucratic quagmire should be cleaned up. Limiting class sizes to significantly lower levels would be a great step in the right direction.

I listened to her comments and sympathized. *It's the same everywhere,* I thought: *Teachers feeling as if they are working in a chaotic and nonsensical system.*

Another new colleague, a special ed teacher, told me that he feels he is no longer a teacher; he is now a case manager, because the bulk of his time must be spent in writing mandatory reports and filling out online forms, plus planning for annual IEP meetings and writing the goals for students. This is another dangerous slippery slope: in an effort to make education equitable for the cognitively affected, the federal government has mandated documentation for IEP's to the extent that the background paperwork and meetings are more important than teaching the child.

In an audit of this SpEd colleague's paperwork a few years ago, the higher ups who came to our school pored over his forms and documents, and never once asked to meet his students or watch him work with them. They were only concerned with the paperwork that would satisfy the law. They visited him in December that year. By March, he was still working on fixing his documentation to their satisfaction and had not worked with a child in all that time. So, the plan he had written in legal documents about giving "90 minutes per week of specialized instruction" did not happen, at all, from December to March.

Current education practices that focus on writing reports
filled with Edu-speak do not help the children
they were supposedly designed to help.
What they do is encourage fraud.

Everyone should see teaching in action!

If you are ever invited to tour an elementary school, try to visit classrooms that are not designated part of the tour. (Remember that third grade colleague whose student population was stacked?)

What you'll notice is that there are a lot of children in each classroom. The teacher can only work with a few at a time, unless she is delivering direct instruction to the entire class, and if you witness one of these lessons, focus on the children more than you do the teacher. How engaged are they with the material she is presenting? You'll probably see a lot of staring into space or doodling on notebooks.

And if the teacher is working with a group at her reading table, there's a good chance that those at their desks are off task. Even if they are sitting quietly with seatwork or at a computer gazing at a screen, you can't be sure how much of the material they are absorbing. Studies by Dr. Tomlinson have shown that children need interaction with adults if they are to grow cognitively. Independent seatwork does not meet that need.

The measure of classroom success is not how quietly the children are sitting, or even if they have a pencil in hand and are looking at a worksheet. The measure of success is how engaged they are. These children fall into two groups, generally: those working with an adult and those mature enough to work on their own. This accounts for perhaps a fourth of the students you are watching.

Regardless of their reason for needing supervision, these other three-fourths are idle for large parts of their day. The fact that no one is guiding them and encouraging them to push themselves means they are spending the bulk of their classroom day in a holding-tank scenario.

Carol Ann Tomlinson's insistence on differentiating for all students is laudable, and it must be our goal. Trying to do that on your own for 30 or even 20 students is an exercise in futility. This is one reason the profession is losing teachers by the thousands. Who would want to do a job that has everything stacked against success, while being lectured that there is no reason it cannot be done?

Chaos:

A state of utter confusion. [3]

Things must change. The question is, how far must we sink before society decides enough is enough?

---

[3] Merriam-Webster Dictionary Online:
https://www.merriam-webster.com/dictionary/chaos

18 Our Model School

The solution to making education effective will require a major overhaul in how we assign personnel to our schools and how we monitor instruction. It will also require helping those currently working in our schools to understand why change is necessary, for everyone's sake — including theirs.

Here is the proposal:

1. Limit elementary class sizes to 20.

This puts kids first in an authentic way rather than a political Edu-speak way. Decreasing the adult-to-child ratio in elementary classrooms is a must if we want our kids to receive a solid education.

According to Kendra Cherry in a piece she wrote for *Very Well Mind,* [1] Jean Piaget postulates in his *Theory of Cognitive Development* that children reach the ability to process language by age 7. Without proper guidance from multiple qualified adults, children are in peril of developing poor language skills that either cannot be overcome or take years to undo. This means that prior to age 7, a child must have the proper phonics instruction that facilitates his ability to attach meaning to symbols. He also must be able to grasp the meanings of *groups of words*, rather than one word at a time. A child who has reached third grade without being able to read independently is now set up for a life of academic failure. His attitude toward learning wanes and his ability to grow cognitively is seriously diminished.

Additionally, a position paper published by the *National Council of Teachers of English* asserts the following:

> Overall, research shows that students in smaller classes perform better in all subjects and on all assessments when compared to their peers in

---

[1] Cherry, Kendra. *The 4 Stages of Cognitive Development: Background and Key Concepts of Piaget's Theory.* 2020

larger classes. In smaller classes students tend to be as much as one to two months ahead in content knowledge, and they score higher on standardized assessments....

... these positive effects of small class sizes are strongest for elementary school students, and they become more powerful and enduring the longer students are in smaller classes. [2]

Almost everyone outside the arena of power and money can see the benefits of relatively small groups of students interacting with multiple adults throughout their school day. It seems only those who do not work in the classroom insist that class size and adult-to-child ratio do not matter.

2. Assign three adults per classroom: one licensed teacher and two highly qualified para-educators. [3]

The adults work together to differentiate instruction for and challenge all their learners. Authentic collaboration is the key, not the masquerade on display now. All children should receive the benefit of being tutored by all the adults, every day.

Teachers and para-educators are assigned students according to their specialties. Advanced learners are identified early and grouped together with teachers trained to work with their abilities. Class groupings are fluid; if children excel faster than anticipated, they can be reassigned to a different group. Likewise, if lagging occurs (meaning more targeted instruction is necessary), class reassignment also occurs. The point is to continually provide students what they *need*, rather than placing them for an entire school year and hoping for the best, regardless of evidence that something must be corrected.

Students with learning difficulties (whether IEP or not) are placed in smaller classes with teachers trained to address their special needs.

One issue with the way we manage teachers is that we assign them to job openings without thought to their strengths, and then we expect them to be good at a job they took because it was the only one available.

When we interview teachers, we should ask them why they want to teach *this specific grade* level or subject. We should also expect only instruction from our classroom teachers. Not counseling, and definitely not behavior management. The distraction of dealing with these other responsibilities seriously affects the quality of instruction delivered. Those who work with

---

[2] "Why Class Size Matters Today." *National Council of Teachers of English,* 2014.
[3] Para-educator: at least two years of college; no teaching license but successful completion of a 'how-to' course offered by the school or district.

children should be hired for their demonstrated abilities for *working with children*, and they should be assigned to classrooms according to what they are good *at*. Their jobs will become easier and more rewarding when counseling and discipline are handled by people who *a)* are very good at it, and *b)* have only *that* task to consider.

3. Reduce Professional Development on a faculty-wide scale.

Conduct these trainings only as necessary, such as for medical purposes and the protocols required to place a child into an IEP.

There are lots of resources available online, and teachers who wish to improve their 'practice' will seek out PD as a team. They can log their trainings in a book.

While voluntary and choice-based PD may seem counter-intuitive to those outside the profession, we teachers know that professional development imposed on us without any apparent need is a waste of money and time. Just ask any teacher in an anonymous survey. While they may sit respectfully through the meetings, they are often resentful. If they participate at all, it's most likely pretense. Training for something you didn't think you needed becomes a wasted hour and can ruin morale. Try to imagine being told in *your* job that you need to improve something that appears not to need improvement. How likely are you to take it seriously?

Consider these words from Matthew Bates, the *Quora.com* writer whom I referenced on page 41:

> You can tell how long a teacher has been teaching by the number of other things they bring to do during mandatory "professional development". That teacher who is front-and-center in the PD meeting, eagerly taking notes and engaging with the presenter? It's their first year teaching. Give them about two more years, and they'll be in the back of the room with the rest of the teachers, grading papers or playing sudoku in such a way as to make it look like they're taking notes. A few years after that, they won't even bother trying to look engaged with the training. They'll be rather open about how much they think that the training is a waste of time.
>
> Unless it's for something practical, like how to use an EpiPen, or how to use a specific computer program, teacher training is a huge waste of time and money. It's actually a pretty good little racket, if you can get in on the presenter side of the action. I did once. I got paid $500 for a two-hour presentation on how to use online classrooms. It was in the middle of the summer in 2019. The teachers who were there were only there because the PD was free, and they needed to earn some

PD credits to keep their licenses. I knew that going into it. I showed them how to use Google Classroom and Edmodo. About 50% of them paid attention for a solid half hour before using the computer that was in front of them to do something else. The other 50% were on their phones from the beginning. [4]

Truer words have rarely been written. No one in authority wants to discuss the realities of human nature when planning professional development. That is a detrimental oversight.

4. Place students in classes according to cognitive ability but also provide other groupings for social-emotional growth.

- Students are placed in their classes and learning groups within those classes according to cognitive development.

It is ironic that the principal I worked for from 2016 to 2018 used this very technique of grouping to create a utopian learning environment for the teacher I described on page 177, including reducing the number of children she worked with and giving her a full-time aide. Of course, his purpose was disingenuous: trying to prove that his idea of best practices works regardless of student load, even while manipulating that load duplicitously. The point is, those in power get it. They understand exactly that optimal learning is made possible through homogeneous grouping, making it all the more frustrating that they continue to eschew this practice.

- Students attend art, music, and PE classes in heterogeneous groups. This means that cognitive ability is not taken into consideration. It also means that some students might leave the teaching classroom for a time while others remain.
- Students eat lunch in heterogeneous groups that are mixed among age levels so the older students can mentor the younger ones. This develops responsibility and empathy.
- Children are supervised at recess by adults trained to interact with them. Play time will include structured games of kickball, softball, and other outdoor sports, in addition to use of playground equipment, like swings and jungle gyms. Many times, students develop sedentary school lifestyles because they do not feel welcome to participate in outdoor activities. Structuring these activities with an adult to supervise helps defeat that possibility. The adults who supervise recess will not be the

---

[4] Bates, Matthew on Quora.com: "What must schools prioritize to better address the needs of students in the 21st century?", 2022.

same para-educators who work in the classrooms. (That is a different skill set.) They can be assigned as an adjunct of the P.E. teachers and receive support from that department for their playground activities. Recess should be a supported way to socialize, get physical activity, unwind, and rejuvenate; and in my school, playground activities will run most of the day, rotationally. This allows children to be outside in small groups.

5. Do not require teachers to create learning goals for their students.

Implement this exercise instead:

- Give intermediate (4-6 grade) students their individual state test scores from the previous school year. Guide them to set their own learning goals.
- Let students know that how they perform on these goals will affect their instructional placement. They will be put in classes that address their needs. Parents and guardians will be included in this process.
- Testing from agencies like NWEA and ITBS can also be used to place students in classrooms and programs. This should be made clear to both students and their parents.
- Finally, a child's past achievements in the classroom will also affect his future class placements.

These points affect student buy-in, a necessary piece in the education machine. An adjunct of that is how principals present testing and progress-monitoring to guardians, who must be strongly advised that their child's education is a product of his own choices.

As Melissa Williams pointed out on page 179, goals are the driving force in education. When used appropriately for student motivation, goals *can* affect student achievement remarkably.

6. Install CCT (Closed Circuit Television) cameras in each classroom.

Students and their parents will understand that poor behavior will be immediately addressed, and no student will be permitted to ruin learning for anyone else.

CCT cameras are a critical component for combatting student malaise and poor choices, as well as proving to parents the demeanor of their child in the classroom. Currently, argumentative parents can (and do) disturb the serenity of a school, as principals are unwilling to fuss with them about what was reported by the teacher. Most parents are not argumentative, but enough *are* that it poses a problem for everyone. The same can be said about students: most may be well-behaved, but those who *aren't* suck the oxygen out of a learning environment.

Students who make poor behavior choices will be removed from the classroom *immediately* by a discipline team who monitor classroom activities. *Positive Behavior Interventions and Supports* (PBIS) is pointless without real evidence to support the choices kids make. [5] Institute a disciplinary system that has backbone: PBIS will work if the school provides evidence to both the child and parent of behavioral choices. A school's culture should not be determined by *he said/she said* scenarios.

Students will not be able to insist the teacher is targeting him or that he is participating appropriately when he obviously is not. Poor student behavior can be addressed immediately by the dean of discipline and the counseling team, without even involving the teacher in the moment. Removing the drama from disciplinary actions (something that troubled students often thrive on) will help everyone feel comfortable and make better choices. Those troubled students will not be thrust into a detention room for their day; their needs and issues will be addressed by a counselor. They will be put on a plan for improvement and monitored by that counselor. Students who prove consistently that they have issues that cannot be undone by typical behavior management will not be returned to the general classroom. They will receive their education in a separate setting. Of course, they will still join their peer group for non-instructional groupings, such as lunch and recess.

This type of intervention can markedly improve the morale of everyone in the school, especially the other students who become weary from the knowledge that those trying to cause disruption traditionally get most of their teacher's time.

But the use of CCT cameras has another, perhaps even more significant, purpose: observation of teaching performance. Why this idea has not garnered any serious consideration in our modern era of video monitoring of banks, government buildings, businesses, sports venues, and even streets is another testament to the power of the teachers' unions.

In my school, the discipline team will have the job of monitoring the cameras. If a teacher who does not belong in a classroom manages to pass the battery of interviews, he will not last long. Teachers need to understand this from the outset. The unions will not be able to protect them from the consequences of their poor and potentially harmful practices, especially if they are inflicting damage. This is not to say we expect most teachers to fall into this category. What we *do* expect is that a great many of them will fall into the category of not teaching as they claim to be doing. (Removing all the

[5] *PBIS: Everything You Need to Know.* https://ClassCraft.com/pbis. 2022

non-teaching requirements - such as documentation, data collection, and discipline - from their job will make it more likely that those who went into the profession to instruct children and guide independent learning will return happily to those activities.)

I'm sure many will balk at the idea of CCT cameras in a classroom. Why? The idea of cameras alone will help *everyone* make better decisions! Besides, the advent of smart phones means teachers are already susceptible to having their performance filmed; making it official (and regulated) creates a more leveled playing field.

7. Rethink how we hire principals.

Principals are usually hired for two reasons: they were a very successful teacher *and* they were able to impress an interview committee. So we're going to remove the successful teachers from teaching and put them in roles that they may not be very well suited to? The main reason a teacher wants to move to administration is usually the salary, not the job. The principal I worked for from 2005 to 2016 told me once that her only motivation for moving from high school English to administration was the salary. She had loved teaching.

Principals should be chosen for their ability to manage all the moving parts in a school, not because they had success in the classroom. The current practice of promoting successful teachers into administrative positions is a major reason for the chaos in schools. Take the best teachers and promote them into jobs that require a vastly different skill set, and hope they'll be successful. The criteria for being a principal should be one's *ability to manage*. Having a familiarity with what a school *does* and how it *works* is a must, but that type of experience can be gained in other ways.

When we bring outside influences into education, we dispense with the insularity of the enterprise. The director in a non-profit can be a successful principal. So can the CEO of a manufacturing plant. As long as these folks secured an advanced degree in education administration, their lack of teaching experience should not be a hindrance to getting the job, because they will no longer be evaluating teachers (see point 9.). Any principal who wants to be successful would make it his mission to find out everything about every job within a school by shadowing those personnel at various times throughout the school year.

Regarding the non-teaching support personnel in a school, highly paid assistant principals are a waste of money. Their job usually consists of coordinating fundraising, planning professional development, administering discipline, evaluating teachers, and covering when the principal is off-site. We don't need to pay someone one and a half times the salary of a teacher for these services that are often done by someone else anyway. (And some of these activities, like fundraising, can be jettisoned altogether.) Instead, we'll have a principal's executive assistant who will coordinate the activities of everyone else working in the school, reporting to the second in command, the dean of discipline, when the principal is off-site.

The *everyone else* I refer to will be those people who are hired as support personnel: a counseling team, a guardian advisor whose job is to address parent concerns, and subject specific specialists who will provide support *as requested* from the classroom teachers. The crucial difference between these specialists and an assistant principal is that they will not have supervisory status over teachers. This is necessary if we want the faculty to work together as colleagues for the benefit of all their students.

8. Remove the principal as the sole evaluator of teaching performance.

Currently, the principal is considered the master teacher in any school. He is considered the most qualified to teach and give advice to teachers, as well as hold them accountable for their performance.

Why?

What makes him the best educator in the building? He may have been a great teacher prior to becoming a principal, but the likelihood is that he's been out of the classroom for many years. (And if he was a high school teacher promoted to be principal in an elementary school, he certainly is not the best educator in *that* building.) Veteran teachers who are still in the classroom are more qualified to assess a teacher's methods than the principal, although I don't advise that, either. My plan for teacher evaluation appears in point 9.

When we eliminate the notion of the principal as the supreme arbiter of what works with students, we free her up to run the school effectively. She still needs to attend district meetings, write reports, allocate the budget and other resources in the school, hire qualified people, and chair whatever committees are deemed necessary. (Be careful about this, however. Forming committees just to say you did is the slippery slope to more bureaucracy.)

And finally, let's stop kidding ourselves about the politics in school. Teachers on the fast-track spend a lot of time and energy trying to butter up their superiors. This undercuts the mission to provide what students need.

Additionally, our current system allows for massive power grabs to be played out between administrators and their teachers. It is very easy to entertain oneself as a principal or (more likely) an assistant principal by putting your least favorite teachers through the ringer.

Likewise, it is very easy to catapult oneself to stardom simply through becoming a yes-man. Without the incentive of sucking up to achieve a favored status, teachers will be more likely to concentrate on the job they were hired to do.

9. Make teacher evaluation the purview of a committee.

This committee can be comprised of the subject specialists, community leaders, and selected parents, all of whom will have access to the CCT feed in real time. (Additionally, our foundation's Board of Directors will have unlimited access to the feed.) Any teacher should operate with the understanding that her instruction will be viewed by an evaluation committee. Using currently available technology, members can log into a system and record their observations, concerns, and suggestions without consulting with each other. (This is an ideal and appropriate use of an NDA: committee members should not be discussing their observations with *anyone*. We don't want to add a different kind of sucking-up to the evaluation process.) Teaching teams will be able to read these ideas at will, without knowing who posted them. In this way, they can address concerns themselves and work on ways to improve classroom practices.

Evaluation will be more effective as an ongoing process than the current method of a principal walking into a classroom to observe teaching perhaps three times a year. If teaching teams and support personnel are continuously working on ways to improve instruction and expectations for learners, there is no need for goal setting, data collection (that means nothing, really), or narrative-writing by principals as they fill out their end-of-year reports.

Belonging to the committee is not a paid position; it's a public service that can later be attached to a resumé. However, participation in evaluation *will* require attending orientation sessions on what effective teaching looks like, as well as counseling about the mission and its confidential nature.

Assigning a committee of five anonymous persons per teacher will mitigate the likelihood of any teacher being unfairly targeted. The details of this type of evaluation can be hammered out as needed, but the gist should be that classrooms are observed at least weekly by a committee member. Teachers should be counseled that there is no need to feel intimidated; committee members *will* understand the nature of how classrooms work: sometimes there are lessons and sometimes there is only independent work. And sometimes, a teacher *will* sit at her desk and do things, such as reviewing student work or checking email. The mere fact that a counselor will walk into one's classroom and remove a misbehaving child without any fuss will go a long way toward assuaging any feelings of unease.

10. Eliminate the farce of paying teachers according to their advanced degrees, particularly at the elementary level.

Effective teachers do not need a master's degree. Possessing one does not necessarily make someone a better teacher. Exposure to quality teaching and experience at the job do that. I have worked with too many poor teachers who have an M.A. to be fooled into thinking advanced education improves one's level of patience or their techniques and dedication to the job. Reading articles and watching YouTube videos on effective practices will do more for a teacher's ability than gaining an M.A. from an online university, a typical avenue toward salary improvement.

So, what makes a poor teacher, in my opinion? It's usually a person who says all the right things in professional development but 'teaches' through assigning activities rather than instructing students. This person knows how to put on that dog and pony show when she's under observation by the principal, but once that is done, she reverts to business as usual.

Knowing that one's teaching is being viewed regularly will go a long way toward improving classroom practices. A by-product of that is that those who are in the profession for the wrong reasons will no longer have incentive to join it (or stay).

One final thought about how we manage teachers: they should be paid according to a demonstrated ability to work with children. In that sense, a salary schedule is a starting point only. If everyone is paid the same regardless of the value they add to the program, there is no incentive to be excellent at one's job. This practice is a major reason our schools are in the state they are in.

My ideas for this school have been years in the making,
and honed multiple times since I began writing this book in 2019.
Obviously, all elements will be subject to scrutiny and revision
when plans for the school get underway.

What are the upsides to my proposals?

Making teaching transparent via Closed Circuit Television eliminates the need for circular bureaucracy.[6] Public education has been seriously undermined by this debilitating cycle for decades. Holding children accountable for their own achievement on tests makes data worth scrutinizing.

Beyond these obvious points, my plan also addresses the real needs of children. The benefit of additional personnel working with and assessing them in their early school years means that our students can be placed in effective learning groups as they show mastery of material. Diligent instructors can pinpoint – in real time – where a child's deficits lie and address them quickly. An IEP coordinator can be assigned to view classroom activities and then fill out the paperwork required by law. This frees up special ed teachers to continue teaching!

Under this plan, full differentiation is more likely to occur. Think of a fully engaged classroom like the following:

- ✓ Tutoring of kids minus the distraction of monitoring other kids.
- ✓ Kids working online with an adult guiding and keeping them focused.
- ✓ Direct instruction by one adult while the other two troubleshoot learning difficulties among the students
- ✓ Direct instruction in small groups while other students work under the guidance of an adult
- ✓ Eliminated non-productive substitute teacher days. A substitute will still be called in, but she will be directed by the other two adults in the room.
- ✓ Individual conferences with students can now occur as they should—minus the expectation to babysit the rest of the children.
- ✓ Multiple adults interacting with students during project-based learning.
- ✓ Dramatically reduced wasted time.

Let's remember the differentiation ideals of Dr. Tomlinson. Each child's needs and readiness must be planned for and executed effectively. The more

---

[6] Circular bureaucracy: redundant paperwork that begins and ends at the same point, in this case, the federal Department of Education which oversees compliance with federal law and the state departments of education who report to the DoE.

adults who are working with children at the elementary level, the more each child is set up for success later. Improving the adult-to-child ratio *in each classroom* must be a priority. We must reallocate funding to make this happen.

And now ... the hurdles that will need to be overcome:

Cost is likely the first thing my detractors will criticize. Massive expenditures will be necessary to decrease class sizes and increase adult-to-child ratios at the elementary level. Those funds will need to come from somewhere. At present, the power structure has done a pretty good job of convincing the public that a top-heavy machine is necessary for achieving anything in public education. If we can undo that untenable philosophy, we'll be able to allocate this bureaucratic funding in much more productive ways, including building the infrastructure that will be immediately necessary and hiring multiple adults for each classroom.

The cost of the support personnel (dean of discipline and discipline team, counselors, guardian advisor, reading and math specialists) is perhaps something new we must wrap our heads around. But when we eliminate the need to babysit teachers at the district and state levels through complex evaluation systems, we can reallocate those funds as well. Yes, those paper pushers and analysts need to find other jobs, but the employment they were enjoying was unnecessary in the first place.

One last thought about money: If we're going to quibble about the cost of adequately manning our classrooms for optimal learning, then we're not really serious about changing our schools for the better. Most researchers (other than John Hattie) agree that it takes multiple adults working with children to achieve measurable gains with them. Even if they won't admit it outright, ask them about the size of the groups with which they conduct their research. If it's one-on-one or small group, then you've got your answer.

Another critical roadblock will be interference from the teachers' unions. They likely will not approve any plan remotely like this. These unions have historically advocated for business as usual: teachers able to operate in secrecy behind closed doors. This reality is why our lawmakers tried to gain control over teaching through cumbersome evaluation systems. It seemed the only way to mitigate the power that the unions wield.

I became a union rep in my own school in 2001 at the behest of my first principal who could not get anyone else to do the job. (I had become a union member for the first time when I was hired in 1998, buying into their spin that in a district that size, it would be folly not to join.) For two years, I attended monthly meetings and was appalled at the political bent and doublespeak I witnessed. At the end of the second year, I quit the union, so disgusted was I at the insincere façade.

There's a lot these unions don't want the average person to know about them, such as what they really stand for, which is far different than what they express publicly.

Have you ever explored the advertising a teachers' union does for itself, on its own platform? According to its website, the National Education Association (NEA) prioritizes the following activities:

- Is a voice for each and every student;
- Helps teachers achieve professional excellence;
- Advocates for teachers' rights and working conditions; and
- Advances justice. [7]

Our local NEA affiliate always opened the monthly meeting with political items: *advancing justice*, to use their spin. Speakers were brought in at the beginning of every meeting to admonish us about the correct way to think and talk about education, or to campaign and ask for volunteers. Sitting through these sessions was excruciating.

Regarding the first two bullet points, never once in those meetings did I hear anyone talk about what our students need or how we could "*achieve professional excellence*". A fly on the wall wouldn't have been able to tell that this was a meeting of teachers!

I did, however, hear a lot about our *rights*:

Advocating for teachers' rights is an extreme example of bending language to suit an agenda. What *rights* are we talking about? The right to work in a safe environment, free from hazards? The right to fair compensation that includes benefits like health care and retirement planning? The right to freedom from workplace bullying? These are the kind of rights most employees think of when you mention that word.

But no. Our union talked about the right to keep our job regardless of how we performed it, and how to posture during the probationary period so every member could reach that magical non-probationary stage, the one where we couldn't be fired for any reason other than criminal behavior. The right to have duties within our school assigned according to seniority rather than

---

[7] National Education Association. https://www.nea.org/

ability. The right to a fair distribution of students among classrooms. And finally, the right to never be required to do more than obligated by the master contract.

Every meeting sounded like every other. And it always ended with reminders that those who are not members are 'leeches', latching unfairly onto *our* efforts to create an equitable workplace. This involved counseling us on how to harangue non-members at our school about enjoying the benefits of collective bargaining without contributing monetarily to the process. Think about what collective bargaining means, however. It is not just the salary schedule, which I shared and discussed on page 148; you know how I regard *that*.

It's also every aspect of employment, including assigning a teacher's documentation biblical status and making all class groups equitable for teachers. Even caps on class size are negotiated by the union. Based on how those caps in my school were placed very high for some grade levels but much lower for others, I believe there are unsavory and/or unscrupulous deals being made regarding the interpretation of class size. This must be how our sixth-grade classes routinely had 32 to 35 students each, while the seventh and eighth grade teachers enjoyed class sizes of 17 to 22.

When I visited the NEA's website recently (nea.org), I saw that they've upped the ante on gaslighting. [8] Everything on this site is designed to make the public think NEA's primary purpose is to improve education through offering teachers avenues toward self-improvement. (They also try to persuade us that school choice and vouchers will destroy that process. The only thing school choice will destroy is the union's ability to control public education. Common sense – and history – tell us that when *choice* affects funding, everyone improves out of necessity for survival.)

NEA.org also tries to sell us on how much they do for students and that just *being* a teacher means you're invaluable. (That's like saying 'Just *being* a restaurant means you're five-star'.) Having been a member as well as a school rep, I'm not buying it. Teachers' unions may 'protect' the good teachers (and *protect* is stretching it), but they also protect the bad ones. Every horrible teacher I have worked with was also a staunch supporter of the union and made public comments parroting the union party line: *'If you're not a member, you're a leech.'*

---

[8] Gaslighting: manipulation through the use of language to cause doubt and second guessing, despite ample evidence to the contrary.

At my school in Colorado, fewer than 10 of the nearly 50 teachers were union members until 2012. It was known across our district that if you wanted an easy job with a union to protect you, avoid our school. We always had high scores and a waiting list of parents wanting to expose their children to our rich curriculum and instruction. In fact, our principal at the time (the one who hired me and for whom this book is dedicated) often made the comment that attending our school was like getting a private school education for free. (And no...we were not a charter school.)

To achieve what we were able to, teachers worked very hard, often giving up their non-class time to work with children, such as before school, during lunch, and even after school. No one was paid extra for any of this; teachers just offered it because they cared about giving help to those who either needed it or wanted it. The teacher I spoke of in chapter 1, the lady whose presence we all endured for ten years (see page 8), was one of those staunch union activists and often made little speeches in our breakroom about how it's unacceptable to expect teachers to work with kids beyond what is required by contract, and that anyone who did it without demanding extra pay was foolish. Her demeanor was a drag on everyone, but no one called her out for it. Everyone just smiled noncommittally and shrugged.

After the new evaluation procedures were rolled out, the number of union members in our school began to steadily increase. On page 129, I wrote about the schism that develops between principals and their teachers when collegial bonds are broken. That's what SB 10-191 did, and the result is that many teachers became union members as a defensive maneuver. By the time I retired in 2018, three-quarters of the teachers in my school belonged to the NEA's local affiliate. So do *you* think the unions decry poor legislation? I seriously doubt it. Their most powerful ingredient for success is making teachers feel like victims in their profession. There *has* to be a better way to compensate quality teachers for what they do.

One last thought about unions: they may say they advocate for teachers, but more than one colleague has told me over the years that they couldn't get the union to assist with a problem. One recent colleague told me that when she had an issue with her principal, she was told by her union that they couldn't help her because membership at her school was only at 20%. Increase the membership, they said, and we'll see what we can do. Instead, she was inspired to cancel her own membership.

Earlier in this book, I wrote about field-testing policy ideas before making them permanent. I propose that my model school becomes a field test. Then let's see how much the unions want to continue their protestations of righteousness.

Think of the long-term implications of what I propose. No longer will teachers and administrators be perpetrating a veneer of effective education; they will be delivering it!

This, or something similar, must be the wave of the future, if we are to educate our children to address the world as it evolves around them.

To be fair, it is not only the unions who will balk at my proposals. Teachers do not want to give up the sanctity of their private realms.

Most teachers will tell you that the worst part of their job is how bureaucracy has taken over every aspect of it, but they are unwilling to change how they view the classroom setting. Working in teams and allowing cameras in will not appeal to most of them. Neither will an evaluation system that involves public and parent input.

But that bias is to their detriment.

Non-teaching requirements will only get more onerous in the future, as politicians continue their knee-jerk reactions and education elites continue to propagate implausible theories for teacher and protocol improvement, while everyone ignores the final leg on that stool: the responsibility of the *child* for learning. Additionally, student and parent poor behaviors will continue to escalate in our litigious society.

Our current predicament, in which it has become *more important to document* teaching tasks and their supposed outcomes *than to teach*, must be resolved.

- Pretending that effective differentiation can occur with a ratio of one adult to thirty or more children is disingenuous.
- Requiring more non-teaching duties for teachers will not make differentiation any more doable.
- Whitewashing fraudulent practices does not obfuscate their reality.
- More bureaucracy will not fix the problem.

We need an overhaul in the way we view and manage education.

There are a lot of hurdles to fixing our broken system: it will be the most difficult challenge in our lifetime.

One major hurdle is the ongoing theory that an egalitarian education means we should ignore factors like effort, ability, and motivation, even though these traits have proven to be valuable in all aspects of a successful life. The powers-that-be insist upon placing most children in heterogeneous class groupings and ignoring competence when assigning teachers to those groups. Dispensing with these illogical practices will push us ever closer to what *should* be our goal: making education work *for students*.

The principle of equal *opportunities* for all students must be preserved. The prevailing union principle of *equity* for teachers must be jettisoned. Equal outcomes cannot be preset, for either students *or* teachers. Policies that dictate these identical outcomes, regardless of ability, effort, or achievement, encourage mediocrity. We must do better.

> The biggest hurdle, however, is the traditional idea of
> what public education is: one teacher, 30 students,
> and the hope that most of the children
> will have a good year.

There are millions of reasons to change our trajectory. Every child in every school represents one of those reasons.

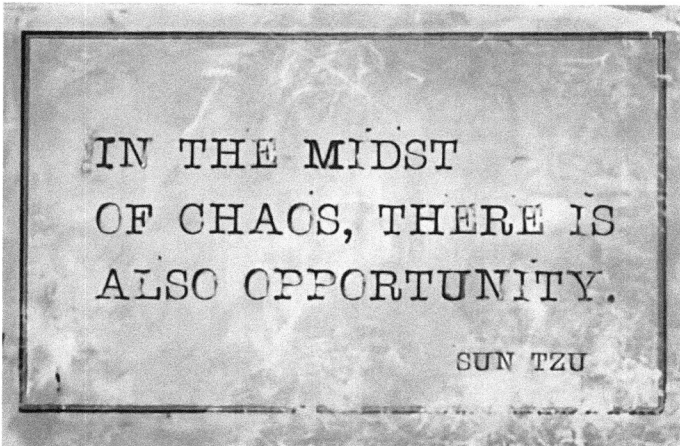

IN THE MIDST
OF CHAOS, THERE IS
ALSO OPPORTUNITY.

SUN TZU

School Matters Foundation
Because educating kids effectively is everything.

Final Thoughts

My ideas about education began forming when I entered college in 1981. At that time, the tide was just beginning to shift toward requiring greater accountability from teachers. It was an uphill battle, as the teachers' unions represented staunch resistance. As a layperson just beginning the journey toward teacher-hood, I saw that the position the unions took could cause PR issues between teachers and the public. When an organization is perceived as protecting even those members not fit for the job from involuntary separation from the profession, the public gravitates toward cynicism.

From my perspective, the unions have worked tirelessly over many decades to create a veneer that their existence ensures quality in education. This could not be further from the truth. Their existence ensures that the power structure will continue to enact feeble measures in pursuit of a veneer of their own: that legislation positively affects education.

A teachers' union is not the same as a blue-collar labor union. The results of poor teaching have long-lasting detrimental implications for society. Because of masterful marketing, however, the teachers' unions have managed to present themselves as essential to the safety of teachers, in much the same way the United Auto Workers or United Steelworkers are for *their* members. As a result, we're all caught in a conundrum that has become insurmountable: the AFT and NEA are so powerful, it is impossible to enact measures that compel teachers to do their job well, all the time. Caveats and exemptions to every policy are inevitable.

No Child Left Behind may have been an admirable attempt to circumvent this power, but it was doomed from the start. There was no way legislation was going to inhibit a teacher's ability to operate in private behind closed doors. The *Every Student Succeeds Act* only exacerbated the situation by turning accountability into interpretational art.

When Colorado enacted its own mandates in 2011, many, many people believed they were union-proof; legislation would finally accomplish accountability in education. I believe these people operated from a regrettable stance of naiveté. The unions may not have been able to thwart the passage of SB 10-191, but they were extremely successful in figuring out how to control the new evaluation systems. Billions of dollars have been spent in Colorado creating evaluation protocols that do little more than affect a façade of competence.

Part of that façade is the concept of Highly Qualified Teachers, a recurring theme in education for decades. How a teacher is determined to be highly qualified, however, is a controversy of its own. The unions, and even education elites, insist that possession of a master's degree plays a major role in making one highly qualified to teach. This is a flawed concept, similar to the supposition that reading a biography of Lance Armstrong, even multiple times, qualifies one for the Tour de France. A master's degree can enhance a teacher's background knowledge, but it does nothing to ensure that one can or will use the skills necessary to unleash a child's intellect, or that one will even have the patience to persist. Unfortunately, it looks good on paper for a district to be able to claim a high percentage of master's degrees among its teachers. The fact that it does not matter what discipline that degree is in should ring alarm bells.

While NCLB was largely abandoned in 2015 when ESSA took over officially, its stain has been far-reaching. The idea that documentation and data collection can be used to accurately assess schools, school districts, teachers, and students persists in every aspect of education today. "Look at the data" everyone says. But that data can be skewed, both lawfully and unlawfully.

Analysts have written extensively about NCLB and ESSA, with articles and op-eds featured on websites such as EdWeek.org, Understood.org, Brookings.edu, and NPR.org. From my research, however, I find that very few of them examine the chasm between mandates and implementation. Here is where we come full circle back to where we started: it is still true that teachers can operate in private behind closed doors, regardless of how many stipulations are placed on them, and that their documentation usurps other evidence that they might not be qualified, let alone *highly qualified*, to teach. Therein lies the rub. It doesn't matter how much legislation is enacted to try to force quality in education. As long as the unions control the show, it will all continue to be window dressing only. SB 10-191, like NCLB and ESSA before it, is 'feel-good' legislation. It has no backbone.

The solution must be to break the power the unions hold. We need cameras in our classrooms, for starters, both to ensure quality instruction and to make that instruction easier for teachers to carry out. Secondly, we must jettison the practice of single evaluator ratings on teachers. My plan to institute committee evaluations will undo corruption at the school level.

And thirdly, we must reduce the teacher-to-child ratios in our schools. **The billions that have been poured into education in the form of materials and strategies have not netted a significant improvement in achievement.** This fact should have alerted authorities years ago that these things don't make the difference. The people who work with children make the difference. The shift should be toward increasing adult-to-child ratios *in each classroom*. Why is this such a non-starter? Because working in teams means that teachers can no longer rely on paperwork to gain a favorable review on performance.

This is not to say that most teachers have nefarious motives. Not at all. Many of them have simply adapted to the changing times: over the last twenty years, **teaching as a profession** in which the participants are rewarded handsomely for their part in the bureaucracy has usurped the concept of **teaching as the means** to a solid education *for students*. This shift must reverse itself if we are to save public education.

Change is a difficult thing, but we must learn how to embrace it if we are to save our failing schools. The cost of continuing business as usual is too high.

As I wrote in the *Foreword* of this book, there are plenty of experts out there who will likely throw bucketfuls of water on my proposals. My hope is that I have provided enough evidence to be convincing in my assertion that the last twenty-five years have been a huge letdown for America's students.

T.L. Zempel

Appendix A

Quality Standards for Rating a Teacher's Job Performance

Professional Preparation

a. Demonstrates accurate, up-to-date knowledge of subject matter.
b. Demonstrates knowledge of how to integrate subject matter and literacy across content areas.
c. Implements research-based best practices in instruction.
d. Develops lesson plans incorporating effective lesson design.
e. Plans and implements district-adopted curriculum through alignment of resources and assessments.
f. Aligns content within course and with previous and succeeding grades/courses.

Professional Responsibilities

a. Participates in professional learning opportunities and applies what is learned.
b. Establishes and maintains professional communication, which is clear, responsible, and respectful.
c. Establishes and maintains meaningful two-way communication in a timely manner with students and guardians.
d. Collaborates to accomplish team, school, and district goals and practices.
e. Maintains up-to-date records of student progress according to District policy and school norms

Professional Practices

a. Communicates to students the expectations for learning.
b. Models and facilitates higher-level thinking, problem-solving, creativity, and flexibility.
c. Adapts instruction to meet the instructional needs of all students.
d. Administers all building, District, and State assessments with fidelity.
e. Provides varied opportunities for student demonstration of learning.
f. Provides meaningful and constructive feedback to students.
g. Uses a variety of formative and summative assessments to make instructional decisions.
h. Explicitly communicates criteria for student success.
i. Develops a safe and welcoming learning environment.
j. Develops relationships with students that foster a culturally responsive learning environment.
k. Collaboratively develops, models, and communicates clear expectations for student behavior within a learning environment.
l. Develops and carries out appropriate consequences in the classroom.
m. Maximizes available instructional time
n. Implements classroom and building rules and procedures.

Appendix B

The Non-Disclosure Part of An Ethics Agreement
Circa 2013

All employees should be alert for any indication of fraud, financial impropriety or irregularity within his/her areas of responsibility.

Fraud includes but is not limited to:
- Forgery, unauthorized alteration of any document or account;
- Misappropriation of funds, securities, supplies or other assets, including   theft, embezzlement, purchasing property for personal use and providing false information to obtain material benefit.
- Unauthorized use of district equipment, facilities, supplies or funds for purposes unrelated to district business.
- Falsification or manipulation of employee expense records or employee time records.
- Impropriety in handling money or reporting financial transactions. Profiteering because of insider information of district information or activities.
- **Disclosure of confidential and/or proprietary information to outside parties.**
- Acceptance or seeking of anything of material value, other than items used in the normal course of advertising, from contractors, vendors or persons providing services to the district.
- Destruction, removal or inappropriate use of district records, furniture, fixtures, or equipment.
- Failure to provide financial reports to authorized state or local entities. Failure to cooperate fully with financial auditors, investigators or law enforcement.
- Other dishonest or fraudulent acts involving district monies or resources.

Appendix C

Colorado's State Test (CMAS) Scores from 2016 – 2025 [1]

Year	6th grade Percentage of students achieving at or above proficiency on state test		3rd grade Percentage of students achieving at or above proficiency on state test	
2025	23% Math	37% ELA	36% Math	37% ELA
2024	29% Math	44% ELA	42% Math	42% ELA
2023	28% Math	43% ELA	40% Math	40% ELA
2022	26% Math	43% ELA	40% Math	41% ELA
2021	24% Math	----------	---------------	
2020	---------------		---------------	
2019	30% Math	44% ELA	41% Math	41% ELA
2018	30% Math	43% ELA	39% Math	41% ELA
2017	31% Math	41% ELA	40% Math	40% ELA
2016	31% Math	38% ELA	39% Math	38% ELA

Visit SchoolMattersFoundation.org/testing for a sample of the test questions we are using to assess grade level proficiency.

[1] CMAS Test Results: https://www.cde.state.co.us/assessment/cmas-dataandresults-2025

More by this author

Finishing School: An enticing novel inspired by the real events of *CHAOS in our schools*.

What if the potential for subterfuge and corruption goes all the way to the top of the school district? What if school administrators must create their *own* growth goals for teachers and report their *own* unverified data to *their* supervisors? What if the results of this data can either propel an administrator to stardom or doom his career?

Veteran teacher Wendy Taylor is caught up in this what-if world when new assistant principal Gary Morris arrives at her school and decides to label her teaching 'undesirable', despite years of excellent reviews on her performance.

But why? What is Morris' motive for trying to sabotage a teacher who had previously known nothing but success? And why isn't Rebecca, the principal who has known her for seven years, doing anything to stop him?

Intrigue escalates as Wendy tries to stay one step ahead of Morris and save her career. But when she accidentally discovers what's really driving his actions, she makes a decision that changes everything.

Is Wendy prepared to throw away the career she loves for a principle? Find out as she navigates this worst-case scenario of poor policies run amok.

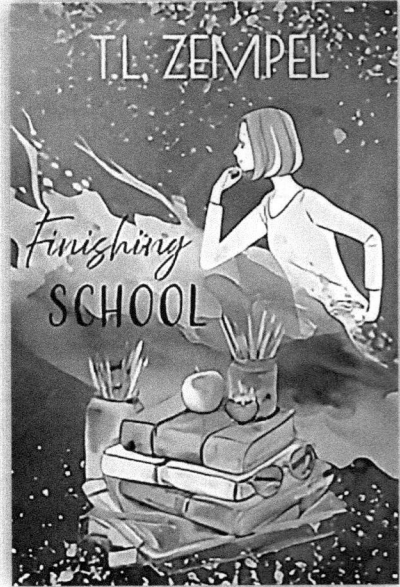

Finishing School is available in paperback and Kindle on Amazon.

From chapter 4: "Used Car Salesman" -

I'm swishing my tea bag in my mug of hot water when Mary suddenly says, "Have you seen the new AP yet?"

"No," I smile. "Have you?"

Nodding, she says, "He was in the office when I picked up my parking pass this morning." She takes a slow sip from her mug. "I heard him telling someone he was an AP at Garfield."

"Garfield!" I'm glad I don't have a mouthful of tea. "What's he doing *here*?"

"Makes ya think, doesn't it?" She smiles slyly at me.

"What did he do to get demoted to an elementary school...?" I say speculatively.

"K-8", Mary corrects. "Don't let George hear you talking like that." Then she says, "Maybe he really wants to be here."

"Who? George or the new AP?"

"The new AP, dummy!" Mary laughs.

I think about the possibility that a high school assistant principal would voluntarily move to a K-8 school. Granted, K-8's have more status than elementaries, but still...

"Why would *anyone* do that? An AP usually only changes schools when he gets promoted to top dog. I mean, don't they all live for the day they can be Number One?"

"That's what *I* always thought," she says, nodding. "Maybe he's hoping for Rebecca's job when she retires."

"Does she look to *you* like she's ready to retire?" I ask dryly, and Mary shakes her head, laughing, and says, "Okay, okay. I concede the point".

"So what does he look like?" I ask. "Is he young? Old? What?"

"He's old-*ish*," she says. "Looks like he's in his mid-fifties."

I smile at her. "Mid-fifties is old-ish to you?"

She grins back. "Oh, right. No offense."

"That's *not* what I meant! I'm not even close yet!" I protest indignantly.

"How many 29th birthdays *have* you had...?" she teases.

"I can't remember," I tell her archly, "but I'm sure only...a few," I say, trailing off.

We grin at each other in our silly girl way.

Then I ask, "So what did you *really* think of him?"

After a moment, she says, "Used-car salesman."

I am grateful for the quantity and quality of
information available online.

These contributors influenced my work tremendously,
and I have done my best to ensure every source
in this book has been given proper credit.

References

A Nation at Risk: The Imperative for Educational Reform. Washington, D.C. The National Commission on Excellence in Education, 1983.

ASCD. *Association for Supervision and Curriculum Development.* https://www.ascd.org/. Accessed 15 Jan. 2022.

Balow, Chris. "The 'Effect Size' in Educational Research: What is it & How to Use it?" *Illuminate Education*, 15 June 2017. https://www.illuminateed.com/blog/2017/06/effect-size-educational-research-use/

Bates, Matthew. "What must schools prioritize to better address the needs of students in the 21st century..." *Quora.com*, 17 Feb. 2022. qr.ae/pvs2B7. "Why do so many people hate Common Core?" *Quora.com*, 15 July 2017. qr.ae/pvs236.

Bergeron, Pierre-Jérôme. "How to engage in pseudoscience with real data: a criticism of John Hattie's arguments in Visible Learning, from the perspective of a statistician." *McGill Journal of Education*, Vol.52, No. 1, 7 July 2017, mje.mcgill.ca/article/view/9475.

Betebenner, D.W. "Growth." *Renaissance EdWords*, 2009, www.renaissance.com/edwords/growth/.

Birr, Chris, and Todd Hrenak. "Using effect size to assess impact: be the 'John Hattie' of your school ." *Elmbrook Schools Winter Newsletter*, School District of Elmbrook, WI, 2015.

Bridich, Sarah Melvoin. "Perceptions Surrounding the Implementation of Colorado Senate Bill 10-191's New Teacher Evaluation. 1 Jan 2013. University of Denver. Free and open access by the Graduate Studies at Digital Commons @ DU: https://digitalcommons.du.edu/cgi/viewcontent.cgi?article=1964&context=etd

Brown, Sarah. "Difference Between Accommodations and Modifications." *Difference Between Similar Terms and Objects*, 27 Aug 2019: http://www.differencebetween.net/language/difference-between-accommodations-and-modifications/.

Cardona-Maguigad, Adriana, and Susie An. "Common Core: Higher Expectation, Flat Results." *NPR Station WBEZ*, 2 Dec. 2019, https://www.wbez.org/education/2019/12/02/common-core-higher-expectations-flat-results.

Cherry, Kendra. "The 4 States of Cognitive Development: Background and Key Concepts of Piaget's Theory." *Very Well Mind*, 31 Mar. 2020, updated, https://www.verywellmind.com/piagets-stages-of-cognitive-development-2795457.

Colorado Department of Education. *4th grade CSAP reading scores*. The Denver Post.com: extras.denverpost.com/testing/400scoresra.htm. 12 Jul 2000.

Colorado Department of Education. *CMAS State Assessment Results*. CDE, 12 Aug. 2021: https://www.cde.state.co.us/assessment/cmas-dataandresults.

31 Jul 2024: https://www.cde.state.co.us/assessment/2024_cmas_ela_math_statesummar yachievementresults.

Colorado Department of Education. *CSAP/TCAP*. 2 Apr. 2020. https://www.cde.state.co.us/assessment/coassess

Colorado Department of Education. *CSAP/TCAP Released Items*. 2 Mar. 2017, updated. https://www.cde.state.co.us/assessment/coassess. Accessed 10 Feb 2022.

Colorado Department of Education. *Senate Bill 10-191*. 23 Oct. 2018. https://www.cde.state.co.us/educatoreffectiveness/overviewofsb191

Colorado Department of Education. *State Model Evaluation System*. 4 Sept. 2019. www.cde.state.co.us/educatoreffectiveness/statemodelevaluationsystem.

Common Core State Standards Initiative. *Grade 6 Math Standards*. http://www.corestandards.org/Math/Content/6/NS/. Accessed 8 Feb. 2022.

Delisle, James R. "Differentiation Doesn't Work." *Education Week*, 6 Jan. 2015. www.edweek.org/teaching-learning/opinion-differentiation-doesnt-work/2015/01.

Dimensions Math. "Exercise 9: Word Problems." Workbook 5A, *Singapore Math*, 2019.

Evans, Mark. "So...What is the Evidence Base?" *Teach It So*, https://www.teachit.so/evidence.htm. Accessed 19 Jan. 2022.

Gewertz, Catherine. "The Common Core Explained." *Education Week*, 30 Sept. 2015. https://www.edweek.org/teaching-learning/the-common-core-explained/2015/09

Garcia, Nic. "From CSAP to PARCC, Here's how Colorado's standardized tests have changed (and what's next)." *Chalkbeat Colorado*, 5 July 2017. co.chalkbeat.org/2017/7/5/21100001/from-csap-to-parcc-here-s-how-colorado-s-standardized-tests-have-changed-and-what-s-next.

Go Test Prep. *Reading Practice Test – Grade 4*. https://gotestprep.com/reading-practice-test-4/. Accessed 8 Mar. 2022.

Go Test Prep - PARCC. *Math 2019 Grade 4 Released Items*. gotestprep.com/parcc-released-items/. Accessed 10 Mar. 2022.

Hattie, John. "Clearing the Lens: Addressing the Criticisms of the Visible Learning Research." *Corwin Connect*, 22 Jun 2018. https://corwin-connect.com/2018/06/clearing-the-lens-addressing-the-criticisms-of-the-visible-learning-research/

"Learning Targets, Success Criteria and Performance Tasks." *Reeths-Puffer Observation and Evaluation Site.* https://reeths-pufferevaluationsite.weebly.com/uploads/1/3/0/3/13036730/learning_targets_session.pdf. Accessed 1 Feb. 2022.

Mercer Publishing: *Iowa Test Sample Questions.* https://mercerpublishing.com/iowa-assessments/sample-questions. Accessed 23 Dec 2024

NCWIT.org. *8 Ways to Give Students More Effective Feedback Using a Growth Mindset.* National Center for Women & Information Technology. https://ncwit.org/resources/ncwit-tips-8-ways-to-give-students-more-effective-feedback-using-a-growth-mindset/. Accessed 10 Feb. 2022.

OllieOrange2. "John Hattie admits that half of the Statistics in Visible Learning are wrong." *OllieOrange2 Blog,* Part 1: 25 Aug. 2014; Part 2: 24 Sep 2014. https://www.ollieorange2.wordpress.com/2014/08/25/people-who-think-probabilities-can-be-negative-shouldnt-write-books-on-statistics/.

OSPI. "No Child Left Behind." *Washington Office of Superintendent of Public Instruction,* https://www.k12.wa.us/policy-funding/grants-grant-management/every-student-succeeds-act-essa-implementation. Accessed 1 Feb. 2022.

Paul, Catherine. "Elementary and Secondary Education Act of 1965." *Social Welfare History Project: Virginia Commonwealth University,* VCU Libraries. https://socialwelfare.library.vcu.edu/programs/education/elementary-and-secondary-education-act-of-1965/. Accessed 15 Jan. 2022.

Pollack, Jane E. "How Feedback Leads to Engagement." *ASCD,* Association for Supervision and Curriculum Development, 1 Sept. 2012. www.ascd.org/el/articles/how-feedback-leads-to-engagement.

The Power of Believing That You Can Improve. Carol Dweck. *TED: Ideas Worth Spreading,* Nov. 2014. www.ted.com/talks/carol_dweck_the_power_of_believing_that_you_can_improve.

"Prepare for Your Teaching Career with the Praxis Tests." *ETS: Educational Testing Service,* ETS, www.ets.org/praxis. Accessed 15 Jan. 2022.

Psychology Today. "Growth Mindset." https://www.psychologytoday.com/us/basics/growth-mindset. Accessed 15 Jan. 2022.

Ritchhart, Ron, et al. *Making Thinking Visible: How to Promote Engagement, Understanding, and Independence for All Learners.* Foreword by David Perkins. Jossey-Bass, a Wiley Imprint, 2011.

Robinson, Sheila B., Ed.D. "Teacher Evaluation: why it matters and how we can do better." *Frontline Education,* www.frontlineeducation.com/teacher-evaluation/#teacher-eval. Accessed 15 Mar. 2022.

Silver, Harvey F., et al. *The Core Six: Essential Strategies for Achieving Excellence with the Common Core.* Paperback ed., Association for Curriculum and Supervision Development, 2012.

Slavin, Robert. "John Hattie is wrong." *Robert Slavin's Blog*, 21 June 2018. robertslavinsblog.wordpress.com/2018/06/21/john-hattie-is-wrong/.

Spectrum. *Reading: 3rd Grade.* An Imprint of Carson Dellosa Education, 2015.

Test-Guide. *Iowa 5th Grade Math Practice Test.* https://www.test-guide.com/quizzes/iowa-5th-grade-math-practice-test#google_vignette. Accessed 23 Dec 2024.

Test Prep Online. *NWEA MAP Test: Math Section Practice.* https://www.testprep-online.com/map-math-practice. Accessed 10 Feb. 2022.

TestingMom.com: *Iowa Assessment and ITBS Test (Iowa Tests of Basic Skills).* https://www.testingmom.com/tests/itbs-test/. Accessed 23 Dec 2024.

Tomlinson, Carol Ann. *Fulfilling the Promise of the Differentiated Classroom: Strategies and Tools for Responsive Teaching.* Paperback ed., Association for Supervision and Curriculum Development, 2003.

U.S. Department of Education. *ESEA Flexibility.* www2.ed.gov/policy/elsec/guid/esea-flexibility/index.html. Accessed 10 Jan. 2022.

U.S. Department of Education. *No Child Left Behind.* www2.ed.gov/nclb/landing.jhtml. Accessed 10 Jan. 2022.

Visible Learning. Sebastian Waack, visible-learning.org/about-visible-learning/. Accessed 15 Jan. 2022.

Watson, Michael. "Student Growth Measures: What We've Been Missing." *Phi Delta Kappan: The Professional Journal for Educators*, 25 Nov. 2019. kappanonline.org/student-growth-measures-assessments-watson/.

"Why Class Size Matters Today." *National Council of Teachers of English.* NCTE, 1 Apr. 2014. https://ncte.org/statement/why-class-size-matters/.

Wikipedia. *Adequate Yearly Progress.* en.wikipedia.org/wiki/Adequate_Yearly_Progress. Accessed 10 Feb. 2022.

Wikipedia. *Association for Supervision and Curriculum Development.* en.wikipedia.org/wiki/Association_for_Supervision_and_Curriculum_Development. Accessed 10 Feb. 2022.

Wikipedia. *Individualized Education Program.* en.wikipedia.org/wiki/Individualized_Education_Program. Accessed 16 Jan. 2022.

Williams, Melissa. "What Are the Best Practices in Teaching?" *ClassCraft*, 9 Oct. 2019. https://www.classcraft.com/blog/teaching-best-practices/. Accessed 15 Jan 2022. Current site: https://www.hmhco.com/people/melissa-williams

www.ingramcontent.com/pod-product-compliance
Lightning Source LLC
LaVergne TN
LVHW052019080426
835513LV00018B/2083